I'M A CHRISTIAN BUT...

KINGSWAY PUBLICATIONS
EASTBOURNE

First published 1980

ISBN 0 86065 081 2

Printed in Great Britain for
KINGSWAY PUBLICATIONS LTD
Lottbridge Drove, Eastbourne, E. Sussex BN23 6NT by
Fletcher & Son Ltd, Norwich

Contents

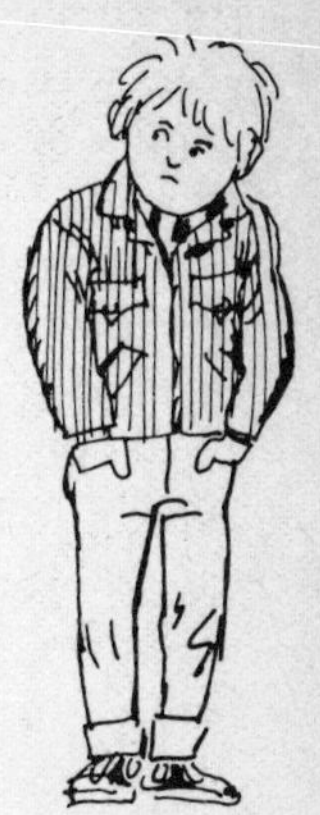

...People laugh at me

Phase One. Why do people laugh at you? Well, basically it's because *you* are scared of *them*!

I know, I know, not everybody can be the 'life and soul of the party' type—but you must have some kind of confidence or people will always laugh at you!

It's a gut-feeling that people get, a feeling you've had yourself when you've felt that someone specifically was 'making up' to you. Take dogs for instance. If you're walking down a street and suddenly there's a hunking great St Bernard looking down at you, that dog is going to know if you're frightened of it. And if you are, it's going to growl and bark and if it decides you're frightened enough—it might even bite you! But on the other hand, if you like dogs, you can look it straight in the eye, smile maybe and walk right past, or even stop and say hello. The reaction from that same dog will be totally different. There's a great possibility that it will smile back, dribble and roll over and wait for you to tickle its tummy. Dogs know if you like them, or if you're afraid.

Humans are just the same. We all know the difference between 'being nice' and 'meaning it', and those kids you're trying to share the gospel with know it too. If you are afraid that they are going to laugh at you, then they *are* going to laugh at you just as sure as the dog is going to bite!

Let's get one thing straight. They won't be laughing at Jesus. They'll be laughing at you making Jesus into something highly embarrassing and uncomfortable. They won't see anything in Christianity if you are going to be pathetic. For your classmates or workmates, the world is a place where people let them down, where everything's a lie and nothing lasts for ever. You have got to come over to them with the confidence that is yours because of the salvation you've found in Jesus Christ.

When our gospel group first started taking assemblies at schools, we felt very out of our depth. We would set up our equipment on the assembly stage and stand looking bewildered and lost, not to mention a bit perturbed at the 700 or so schoolkids filing in. Then you'd gradually hear people whispering, 'Do they do punk? . . . rock band . . . what is it? . . . this should be a laugh . . . !' And gradually you'd find yourself thinking 'My life! They think we're a heavy group, and we're not, no way, we're very pop! They're gonna hate this, it's a disaster before we start!'

Now all these feelings were being perfectly portrayed on our faces and the kids could already feel that we were not certain of ourselves any more. And the sniggering would continue throughout the performance. Well, we had to put up with that until we gradually found our feet and grew more confident, and once we were more confident—the boot was on the other foot! Now we had a group that wouldn't stand any messing around, that knew at a nod of a head or wave of the hand exactly what to do. And the schoolkids gave us new respect! They appreciated the professionalism and listened to every word we sang or said.

And once *you* know what you are talking about, then people will listen to what you have to say, without laughing or jeering at you. So before we go any further, we'd better take a little look at the way you're going about your own Christian life.

There's nothing worse than listening to someone who doesn't know what they're talking about, or *who* they're talking about, come to that. You know the sort of thing. . . .

'I know David Essex. Well, actually I know his mum; well really his mum knows my friend's aunt.'

Not very impressive, is it?

Well, how well do you know Jesus? Because a lot of how you're going to get on with your friends will lie on how well you know your subject. And you know and I know that the only way you'll get to know Jesus is to spend time with him. I don't really think it needs spelling out too much, as just about every question in this book will really boil down to how well you, personally, know the Lord. Are you spending enough time with him? Is he real to you? When was the last time the Lord answered a genuine prayer or need in your life?

When you start telling your friends about Jesus, and how he answers prayer, you will need to back it up with an experience of your own, or once again you will find yourself the centre of ridicule. But if Jesus is as real as your best friend, you'll have no trouble talking about him to anybody.

But wait your opportunity won't you? Don't go barging in messing up conversations, just take your time and let it come naturally.

Phase Two. On the other hand of course, maybe you are just self-conscious—painfully so. I don't think many people really are, so check it out for yourself before you decide.

If you are painfully shy, then it's not so much a spiritual problem as a personal one. In our group we have six shy people who, on stage, can really get it together and be loud and noisy, but off stage we are all pretty quiet. However, we have one member, Quiddy, who we laugh at a lot, mainly because of his blunders. It's got to the stage where we wait for him to do something wrong! Now that's not fair on Quiddy who doesn't like being laughed at, but as time has gone by, Quid has realized that his having three left elbows is a vital part of his personality, and so he plays on it. He now waits for the audience to applaud if he trips over the mike wire during a song, takes a bow and carries on. Incidentally, the audience loves it!

It's always Quiddy who turns up at the wrong time, wearing the wrong clothes, at the wrong place. It was Quiddy who walked *through* a carpet; it was Quiddy who fell through a chair (on stage, naturally!). Did you chuckle to yourself just then? If you did, it's a natural reaction, and it doesn't mean that people are putting you down! But that is how Quiddy is—and maybe it's how you are, so make the best of your character. We'd hate Quiddy to be any different from how he is, we *like* him like that! So the next time you pick up a cup and are left holding the handle—don't mumble an apology, grin and ask for a round of applause!

Phase Three. 'When the Holy Spirit comes upon you you will be filled with power' (Acts 1:8). Power! Something we all need, and something most of us lack. It is a fact that the Holy Spirit will put power into your life and give you that extra authority to live an extra-ordinary life. (See chapter 12!) But there is another verse that we mustn't overlook. 'The gospel is the *power* of God unto salvation.' The Bible says that when we tell people the good news about Jesus, then they will get saved. The power lies in the gospel—not in you (if you see what I mean). So regardless of the lack of confidence you may have in yourself, people will get saved through your confidence in the gospel! So again, check it out for yourself. See how real God's plan is to you, and then if you are sure that Jesus is alive and living in your heart, well, don't be afraid to tell your friends about it!

We had a night a little while ago when everything was a big disaster. The other girl in Dunamis (that's our group) was ill; one of the boys had lost his voice; and we had to carry on doing a concert. Well, we were absolutely chronic! Chuck broke two strings on his guitar, and while he went to work putting on the new ones three of us had to hold the whole show together. At first we tried to stall it by chatting, but soon we realized we would have to sing. Now when there are usually six voices singing in harmony, plus two guitars, it's a terrible trial singing with three voices plus one guitar! It was one of those nights when you either wanted the floor to open up and swallow you—or the Lord to come back!

We were extremely tired and had nothing going for us at all. It was so bad that we almost couldn't care less, and one of us had to give a chat and an appeal at the end of the evening. We gave the job to Quiddy who was so far gone that he didn't know what day it was. There was no chance of us being bright and breezy—we just felt we had failed miserably and wanted to go home.

So Quiddy got up and in words of one syllable told the kids how Jesus loved them, how he cared enough to die for them. He quoted some verses of Scripture and twenty people became Christians that night! All of a sudden it didn't matter that the group had been lousy, that we had lost our confidence—because the gospel had been given out and people were being born again. And so the Lord proved that he only needs to work through us and it is his word that brings new life, *not* how well

Chuck can play a ten-string guitar!

We went home rejoicing!

And here's one last thought . . . There are an awful lot of Christians who are talented, full of ideas, chatty and good-looking who are sitting around doing nothing for Jesus, simply because they can't be bothered to get up and do it.

Well, God's not asking for ability, he's asking for *avail*ability, and you have got plenty of that!

...I hate church!

'But the church I used to go to was *so* boring, I couldn't stand it!'

That was a comment in a classroom in Derby by a girl who obviously wasn't against going to church, but was just fed up with the impression that particular church had given her.

Sticking a finger in the air, I replied, 'Ah! Now you obviously didn't go to a church where Jesus was proclaimed as alive! When you are in the throes of choosing a church to worship Jesus, look for one with inviting posters outside, ones that say things like 'Happiness is knowing God loves you!' or 'Jesus is alive today!'. If the sign outside the church says 'Grand Jumble Sale on Saturday' then the chances are that jumble sales is what you'll get!'

The girl smiled and nodded, and so did I . . .

unfortunately, the teacher didn't. In fact she frowned, and said, '*We* happen to have a lot of jumble sales in *our* church, but *we* know that Jesus is alive as well!' Yes, but that wasn't really what I was getting at, not at all. I know there are a lot of alive churches who have jumble sales and tap-dancing lessons, etc. etc., but from the point of view of a young person wanting to know about Jesus, it's much more encouraging to see a notice mentioning Jesus Christ than it is a whist drive.

Maybe you're finding this book a little bit different from the norm. That's because I'm trying to be honest with you and understand the situation, which is why the next thing I'm going to say is . . . oh, all right then, I'll admit it, a hair-raising amount of churches *are boring*, with more emphasis on the flower arrangements than the Lord. So let's take a look at some of the reasons.

First and foremost, there's you. What are *you* doing about the situation? Sitting there having a moan, that's not exactly improving the problem, is it? A lot of the time we are to blame for the non-events that so many churches turn out to have. You know what it's like when someone talks about you behind your back. Maybe they're not saying anything too terrible, but you can literally feel the bad vibrations coming off them and on to you. Having felt this sensation, you then let your imagination run riot about the lurid details of some horrible piece of gossip that someone's got hold of and distorted something rotten. Well, it's just the same for our minister, who's preaching a sermon and looks down at you, and you're slumped there with a black cloud hanging threateningly over your head. The preacher's first thought is one of concern for you, and while he's thinking of your problems, he can't concentrate on preaching. Then maybe his second thought is that you don't like his preaching! That immediately makes him worse, and his well-prepared sermon takes a dive! And if there's more than one of you frowning at him, he just doesn't stand a chance. So if this is the case with you, why don't you try being encouraging and smiling at him now and again. Just because he's the man at the front—doesn't mean he's not human . . . like you! Mavbe he would secretly love to frown back!

Secondly there's the whole concept of church and its place in your life. To try and explain how I saw church as a new Christian, I'm going to give you a shortened version of my extremely long testimony. When I was just about to leave school, I had already made up my mind about what kind of job I wanted to do. I wanted to work with pop music, somewhere, anywhere. Not playing or singing, but something glamorous like publicity or press. So when I finally made it to leaving school, I was pretty disillusioned by starting to work in a building society. But I don't give up that easily! While all this was going on, I was still an avid pop fan and constantly writing to the music papers with letters like 'I don't know who's buying records lately but their choice is terrible, the artist must have a lot of relations. . . . ' Or the alternative, 'How come I'm the only person in the world who's bought this record? What's the matter with you all?' Ever so polite I was. In those days I was very into 'soul' music and so most of my letters were praising up one particular record label, and for some reason, a lot of these letters were published, and the end result was that the 'soul' record company that I kept raving on about asked me to go and work for them!

Once you are in the record business, it's quite easy to move around and make contacts and change companies. So I went from Polydor to Atlantic, and from there to RCA, and finally I found myself sitting in the fan club office of Radio Luxembourg. I very much enjoyed my stint at Luxy and there, as in the other places, I met loads and loads of big stars. (Oh yes, I'm probably the only girl in the world who has asked David Bowie who he is!) And among the folk was a songwriter who, like everyone else, was trying to come up with that special song that would go bursting up the charts and make him an overnight success! The guy's name was Tim Rice, and he wrote a small pop opera entitled *Joseph and the Amazing Technicolour Dreamcoat.* I remember going to see the whole thing performed at the Westminster Central Hall in London. It was very different from a lot of the music that was around at the time, and somehow it had that kind of charm that made you like it, whether you wanted to or not! The opera (or was it an oratorio?) was all about Joseph and his coat of many colours. (Now there's a surprise!) I remember thinking to myself, 'Ah yes, there's God. I really must take time out to think about him one day.' And really that's about as far as my thoughts went for the day, and for quite a while after too. I had never doubted that God was there, but I'd never ever considered him as anyone to give much thought to. He was there, holding the world together, and like everybody else, I prayed to him when I got myself into a mess. . . .

Quite a while after this event, Tim wrote another one. This time it was entitled *Jesus Christ Superstar* and it was a full-length pop opera. When the double LP first came out, I must have been one of the first to buy it, mainly because I knew the writer, and because I had loved *Joseph* so much. When you work in the record or radio business, it's hardly ever that you buy an album, because there are so many advance copies for publicity purposes given to you. But I wanted to buy *Superstar* to help it rocket up the charts. . . . (I think it might have just about managed without me buying it, actually).

So *Jesus Christ Superstar* came home with me and found its way to my faithful record player. Now, I don't know about you, but when I buy a new album, I have to play it a million times before I really get into it, and so it was with *Superstar*. The album was very long and hard to grasp after only a few hearings, and so I just kept on playing it and playing it. *Superstar* is a musical centred around the last seven days in the life of Jesus. It's an extremely musical 'musical' and the kind of thing that drives you crazy after a while because you just can't stop singing it. Okay, so now I know that not every word of it was scripturally correct, but that hardly mattered to me at the time. I just got more and more engrossed in the story surrounding the crucifixion.

Can I go off at a tangent for a minute? A while back there was a song called *Matchstalk Men and Matchstalk Cats and Dogs*. That song was all about the artist Lowry. Until that particular time when the record came out, Lowry was just a pretty well-known painter. But as the record reached number one in the pop charts, suddenly the whole world seemed to know about him. Boots and Woolies and places like that began selling those little blocks with Lowry paintings on them. Well, really it was the same with me and Superstar. Jesus had suddenly been brought to my attention and I realized that I didn't know much about him, and I wasn't really sure who to ask. Church was not my immediate thought, because I wanted to ask a *person* not (as I viewed the church) a building. So I asked around my friends and contacted people that I thought of as 'religious', but none of them really seemed able to help. By the time I had searched and searched for someone to tell me about the 'real Jesus', I was beginning to get a few hang-ups on what was in store for me, should I become a Christian. Going back to the album for a minute, there were two songs that were beginning to worry me.

One was about Pilate. Pilate was a governor who quite liked Jesus. In fact, he couldn't really see anything wrong with him, but Jesus was standing on one side of his life, and on the other side was this large jeering mob. Not wanting to endure the mob, Pilate turned his back on Jesus. . . .

But then, there was also Herod. Now, Herod was King. Well, he had heard that people were going around calling Jesus the King—which is definitely not on when you are king yourself. As far as Herod was concerned, Herod ruled OK, and while *he* was around, there wasn't going to be another king. Jesus or no Jesus.

The first song, the one about Pilate, was bugging me, because I thought, 'If I become a Christian (and I was in grave danger of doing so) then I'm going to step over to Jesus' side, and if I go to Radio Luxembourg (which was where I worked at the time) and tell my workmates I'm a Christian then they will probably fall about laughing and I will come in for a fair amount of jeering. Oh! they might even tell me to leave!' Well, *I* didn't know how the world treated Christians! (Didn't they use to throw them to lions or something?)

And how about this other song—Herod's Song? I already realized that, if I became a Christian, God was going to do some taking over. He might say to me 'Sorry Sue, you can't work at Luxy any more, I want you to go and work in the local butchers.' That would be awful! Not so much working in a butchers, but not having any say in what turnings my life took.

My final thought on the matter was one of Christians and church. I had always had a clear picture in my mind of what a Christian is. A Christian is someone who has very greasy black hair, parted in the middle, wears very thick pebble glasses, has spots, wears black all the time, never laughs and only breathes when necessary—and I knew I didn't want to be that kind of person. And if that was a Christian, then church must be the draggiest place in the world. (Can you imagine masses of people wearing black, and frowning, all under one roof?)

Unfortunately, after giving up trying to find out about Jesus through acquaintances, I did finally put my dirty white plimsolls inside a church. And surprise! surprise! Someone shook hands with me and made me very welcome, gave me a book and showed me to my seat. That usher will never know what a good job he did that day, because I was very ready to bolt out of the door should church have been as I imagined it.

To cut a long story short, I heard the gospel that night and realized that all the suffering that was so well portrayed on my LP was a fact, and that Jesus went through all that suffering for me. I heard that Jesus died for me and that in return I could give my life to him. But as much as I realized that I could become a Christian, it was weeks, maybe months, before it really all sank in. It took me a long while to settle into a church, as the real value of it was still fuzzy in my head—as were a lot of things relating to Jesus. When you first get saved, you don't automatically know everything. You pick up little bits at a time. The first thing I really appreciated was talking to Jesus as a friend and the creator of Essex where I lived. I would go to work grinning at trees and thinking 'God made that!' I could see the value of prayer—but it was always *me* and the Lord, not me and a *group of people* and the Lord. Things happened step by step. Folk had been telling me I was missing out because I didn't go to Communion. I wouldn't miss a Sunday night, because that was where Jesus' gospel was preached and I could relate to that. But Communion, well, I didn't know what it was, and when I finally went, I felt slightly out on a limb, because in this service people were bobbing up and down every five minutes and praying aloud out of their heads. And I had always thought church prayer was something out of a prayer book.

To be quite honest, it scared me a bit. It seemed so natural to them, but I couldn't have done it to save my life! Perhaps you feel like that now, and perhaps your answer, like mine, is not to rush it. Take your time to get used to one service at your church and understand why you are in that service, so that you can appreciate being there to the full.

I think after that I turned up for Communion once a month, maybe more, just until I could fully comprehend the meaning behind the bread and the wine, and the importance of keeping the only meeting that Jesus specifically told us to keep. But it's hard on a new Christian; no, it's probably more bewildering for at least the first year.

The Bible is a big book, and to understand salvation, redemption, justification, etc. fully doesn't come in a couple of months of gospel meetings. It's like giving a two-day-old baby a motorbike and telling him to pop down the road to buy his dinner and come home and cook it!

So although all the meetings at your church are

important, it would probably benefit you a lot to go to the Bible study more than most. Alas for me, it was the last meeting I got into. I finally made it to the prayer meetings, but Bible studies sounded too much like hard work! However, Bible study was one of the most enjoyable times, because all the secrets and wonders of this fascinating Christian life were being unfolded for me and I was beginning to grow!

So don't worry if you're a young Christian, nobody expects you to be the world's greatest church-goer. Take your time and grow up strong and healthy!

...Does that mean I can't look good any more?

The day my husband John first met me, I was wearing red jeans, a white jumper and a red waistcoat smothered in stickers. My hair was a mass of very curly curls, and I had a little silver star stuck on my face. John was the guest preacher at our church, and I just happened to be giving a testimony. But as far as John is concerned, that's how I looked when he found me, and that's how he likes me to be.

Obviously fashions change, but your personality stays the same and will govern the way you dress.

Before I was married, I dressed to please me, and if I wore something outrageously 'orrible, it would make no difference how many friends and relations told me it looked bad. But somehow, if a total stranger commented on my clothes, *then* I would take notice. I suppose in the back of my mind I would think 'Ah! They are not getting at *me*, because they don't *know* me, so there must be something wrong with this outfit.' I suppose I tended to think people I knew wanted to spoil my fun.

Does that mean I can't look good any more? Depends what you mean by look good! What do you think when you look at yourself in a full-length mirror—just before going out for the evening? . . . Okay, let's put it to the test.

A. . . Am I going to appeal to the opposite sex?

B. . . Do I look sexy?

C. . . Well, it's *so* up to date that it *must* look good . . . I think.

D. . . Yukk! That's boring!

All right, now how did you get on?

A. . . If you're a single person, then probably the most natural question in the world is 'Am I going to appeal to the opposite sex?' And if you're honest, *that* is probably one of the most frequent questions you confront your mirror with. Everybody wants to be appealing. I can see nothing wrong with wanting to look good *but* . . .

B. . . If you slant the same question at the wrong angle it spells danger all the way! It may be very cool to look sexy—but it happens to be an open invitation to anyone who happens to look your way, and it can lead you into no end of trouble! Perhaps you have your eye on one particular fella, girls, but if he's a nice guy, he's not going to want to be seen dead walking around with a girl who looks like she's anybody's! On the other hand, you may see 'dressing to kill' as just a laugh, but to your opponent, it's a green light. And anyway, as a Christian you know it's the wrong attitude. Looking sexy is out! Okay!

C. . . Happily, fashions and trends come quickly and die the same way. The only tragedy being, the money you spent out on those silver-lurex drapes, fellas! You probably only wore them twice.

Fashion is basically fun. But there will always be things that come out which no matter *how* hard you try, are just never going to suit you. No, never. So you will never look good in them. And when this happens, forget it. If it doesn't suit you—don't buy it. Remember the question for this chapter is 'But does that mean I can't look *good* any more?'

D. . . If you think you look boring, you will doubtless become boring while wearing boring clothes. And clothes are a vital part of being young, and like tons of other things, they are very important at the time, so really you are better off wearing the things that you are happy in.

Right, let's carry on. My minister in Barking had a great motto for young people in his church, very simple but neat:—'When in doubt, cut it out.' And that moral code virtually cuts across all the questions asked in this chapter. It's a good code for dress, because deep down *you* know whether what you are wearing is decent or not, and I think that's what counts.

But as far as Christianity goes—well, it's not like joining the scouts: there is no uniform attached to it.

A while ago our group was asked to play for a

month in Scotland. We had been advised to play it very cool regarding the way we dressed as the Scottish Christians were very critical of 'fancy dressing'. So the first Sunday we were there, we had planned to wear what we lovingly refer to as our 'Smarmy gear'. It consists of the boys wearing well-cut light green trousers and light green open neck shirts with posh black velvet jackets, while the girls sported dusty pink blouses, with dark pink velvet trousers and choker to match—all very proper and smooth. Then we hit on a problem.

It seemed that the minister of the church had also booked us to go straight on from the Sunday meeting to a pretty rowdy youth centre in town. Now there was no way that we were going to turn up at a downtown Scottish youth club dressed like that, so we decided we would have to take a change of clothes with us to the church, and explain our position to the congregation. So on the Sunday night we told them the situation and apologized for the fact that we could not stay and chat, and that we would be rushing round the church in our 'scruffy gear' straight after our performance.

Admittedly, it must have looked strange to see the 'smoothies' disappear through the vestry door and then reappear wearing rolled up jeans, boots, white silk shirts, denim waistcoats smothered in badges, red spotted hankies round our throats and flat caps perched cheekily on the sides of our heads!

Reaction? . . . 'Oh, that *does* look smart!' 'Why on earth didn't you wear that tonight?' 'Will you wear it next Sunday?' . . . Most of these comments came from older Christians who could see the effect it would have on unsaved kids—and those who just thought it was more *us*. That evening made me virtually give up on wearing what we thought would make the right impression, and just get on with the job that the Lord had asked us to do.

And secretly, a lot of people would like to dress like you do—you just wouldn't believe the number of ministers that have tried on our gold and silver bomber jackets!

Now I don't expect Christians everywhere to freak out in their taste for clothes, but I really do think it helps if you at least look presentable. I've lost count of the number of times we have visited a school for a concert or assembly, and been met by the dowdiest of teachers or pupils. Even from the car park you can tell that they are Christians! Nobody else would walk around looking like that. Why have Christians got a mental block when it comes to clothes?

You see, you get a school of around 1700 pupils nearly all normal, bopping about, grinning, modern, nicely dressed. And then you get these six individuals who have never heard of combs or brushes, have never been introduced to an iron, and who look at least ten years older than everyone else. They are a big joke to the other 1,694—and they of course make up the Christian Union. Our six-strong C.U. members will tell you they have tried very hard to reach the rest of the school with the gospel, but everyone laughs at them. Can you wonder? Really, can you wonder? It's got nothing to do with the rest of them not wanting Jesus, but it's got a lot to do with not wanting to be associated with a bunch of drips.

Not that Christians have all got ugly faces and figures, it's just that they don't *do* anything with them. For some reason they have no interest in themselves, and I really wish I knew why! Maybe they think that Christians shouldn't attract attention, and that they should fix their eyes only on the Lord and not on themselves. If this is so, then they've taken it too far! I just can't imagine the Lord looking down proudly on someone who can't be bothered to wash their greasy hair!

A lot of this chapter really has nothing to do with being a Christian. It's just that tradition says that it has!

I was talking to a minister's wife a while back and she was going into the realms of 'when I was a young girl, it was considered dreadful to walk into church wearing sheer nylon stockings. Only thick black stockings were considered decent.'

Today, of course, a young girl waltzing down the aisle in black tights would probably get a lot of black looks to go with them! Fashions will always change and re-cycle, and at the moment the fashion editors are trying to coax young girls into wearing hats! Now wouldn't *that* make everyone happy?

...Shouldn't I know what's going on in the world?

A lot of people couldn't care less about our world, but a lot more are very proud of it, and judging by the masses of unions and political parties, I'd say that most people care very much one way or another.

And as a Christian, *you* should care more than the majority.

Probably John 3:16 is the most well known verse in the Bible. It says, 'For God loved the *world* so much that he gave his only Son, so that everyone who believes in him may not die but have eternal life.' God is very concerned that you love the world, and he set us the highest example possible by the sacrificial gift of his son, Jesus.

Don't forget that the world and the people in it were made by God in the first place! I wonder how you view the world? Full of greedy idol worshippers, slanderers, drunkards and thieves? Well, the Bible has a lot to tell you! Let's have a quick look at Paul's description. . . .

'In the letter that I wrote you I told you not to associate with immoral people. *Now I did not mean pagans who are immoral or greedy or are thieves or who worship idols. To avoid them, you would have to get out of the world completely*. What I meant was that you should not associate with a person who calls himself a *brother* but is immoral or greedy or worships idols or is a slanderer or a drunkard or a thief. Don't even sit down to eat with such a person.' (1 Corinthians 5:9-13.) Paul emphatically states that it would be a bad thing for Christians to ignore the world, or not get involved. He doesn't tell us *not* to sit down with such people! He goes on to say, 'After all, it is none of my business to judge outsiders.' In fact, there is so much 'go ahead' given towards going out into the world, that I'm amazed that more people haven't!

It is extremely sad to realize that one of the main reasons there are not so many people going out into the world and preaching the gospel, is that there are far too many weak Christians about. Weak Christians who can't go into a pub to preach the gospel without downing a pint, 'just to show I'm normal' . . . and then the next week they're back again at the invitation of an old friend that they met there, who has managed to persuade the weak Christian that there's nothing wrong with the odd pint. And on face value, that's true. But the idea of going into the pub in the first place was to show your friends that you're *not normal!* You have a life that is so extraordinary and fulfilling that you don't need a pep-up at the end of a busy day!

When Jesus said 'Go into all the world and preach the gospel' he meant just that. He didn't say, 'Go into all the world . . . and forget me.' I've heard too many teenage Christians say, 'I go along to the pub with my friends so that they won't think I'm a bore, and anyway, if I go with them to their pub, then they'll come to church with me!' Great theory, but does it work? How many of your friends have come to church because of the overwhelming impression you made on them by drinking with them? Jesus didn't mean that at all.

We have two extremes. Either Christians don't go out to the world at all, or they go right over the top and mould into the world's shape to such a degree that nobody notices that they're different, and in the end they are swallowed up and they vanish altogether.

A Christian should be salt and light in a rotten dark world. To stop meat going off, you add salt, and to stop darkness being dark, you add light! Dark and dark will only ever add up to more dark! For this reason I shy away from saying, 'Fine! Go ahead, have a party, go to discos, sit in the pub with your mates.' As Paul puts it, we're still suckling on milk and we're not strong enough to take on the world. Oh yes, I know we should be, I adore disco-dancing with my friends, I even went to Saturday Night Fever dance classes, and loved every minute of it . . . but I wouldn't take a

Christian to a disco because somehow it seems to go to their heads and you never get them out again! It shouldn't be like that, but in most cases it is! When Paul talks about having the Spirit of God as opposed to having the spirit of the world, he says this: 'As a matter of fact, my brothers, I could not talk to you as I talk to people who have the Spirit; I had to talk to you as though you belonged to *this world*, as children in the Christian faith. I had to feed you with milk, not solid food, because you were not ready for it. And even now you are not ready for it, because you still live as the people of *this world* live.' (1 Corinthians 3:1-3.) I could probably go further and say that it seems to be a trend to prove to the world that Christians are no different from anyone else!

I had a conversation with a young chap that had a Christian group who were playing in pubs. I was so pleased to find someone else doing this, and asked him how he was getting on with witnessing. He said, 'Oh well, we tell them that we are Christians, and then we just play rock 'n roll to let them see that we are normal guys.' What a let down to anyone sitting in a pub wishing there was more to life!

I know a lot of people would consider our own evangelistic group *Dunamis* terribly worldly, because we wear trendy clothes, sing modern music, own a colour TV and have a collection of over a thousand records! But 'worldly' means that Jesus is not the centre of your life, and that the colour TV etc. comes before your commitment to Jesus. For the Christian there shouldn't be a separation of sacred and secular. Everything we do should be done for Jesus, whether we are praying or playing football. We should be conscious of Jesus in our lives, and live them accordingly. Paul says: 'Someone will say, "I am allowed to do anything." Yes; but not everything is good for you. I could say that I am allowed to do anything, but I am not going to let *anything* make me its slave.' (1 Corinthians 6:12.) So as I said before, although there's nothing wrong with that odd pint, it is all too liable to make a slave of you!

Touchy subject, isn't it? And very difficult to put on paper rather than into practice. As far as living in the world goes . . . I think you should! It's vital that you have an all-round knowledge of what's going on. In our ministry we concentrate very much on young people, and a type of young person that we feel has been left out in the cold for far too long. That is, the young person who belongs to the masses. There are a certain amount of people who have a specialized ministry and that's a good thing. For example, some people feel called to work among sportsmen, some among personalities, and others among politicians, and I feel there is a great need to have men and women in the forefront of these professions that are in fact saved.

In the Christian music scene, it's much the same kind of set-up. People play rock for rock fans, punk for the few punks that are left, folk for folk fans etc., and so this is the way that the rock, punk and folk fans get saved. But what about your average bloke who buys all the records that are constantly in the charts, which consist of a tune you can't let go of and a set of lyrics that you can't help singing? Most people in the world can appreciate a good tune, so if we sing them one, they are going to listen. And if we make our lyrics simple and easy to pick up, then like it or not they will go around singing them!

Confusion has been reigning supreme for quite a while around the Christian music scene, and here it is even more 'chic' to give everyone the impression of normality. The ultimate cool at the moment is to get into 'the secular market'. Can I for a few minutes chat about this much coveted market?

Answer this question honestly. If you had the choice, from a totally *musical* point of view, of going to see a top gospel group, *or* someone like Queen, Abba or Status Quo (depending on your musical tastes), which would you choose? I know that I would choose the secular bands every time! Why? Because, from a musical point of view, they are absolutely miles out in front, and if I want to hear good music, well played, then I turn to the professional secular bands. The point I'm making is this: there are too many Christian groups that are turning their talents towards the secular market and saying things like 'Okay, so I'm a Christian, but I play secular songs, and when I'm famous I'll be in a position to tell people that I'm a Christian.'

Do you want the bad news or the bad news? Bad news number one, there are around 3,000 groups in London alone, all trying to make it—and they're not Christians. Bad news number two, they are all at least as good as you, if not better. So the chances of you becoming a superstar in the first place are not very high!

And what makes you think that you must hide the fact that you're a Christian? Perhaps you think that a song with Christian lyrics would not be acceptable in the charts. . . . You try telling that to Boney M! They've twice made the number one spot with totally Christian lyrics *and* one of them was a well-known scripture chorus!

As a Christian pop group, Dunamis have found that Christian lyrics are accepted everywhere, in pubs, clubs, bingo halls, schools, prisons, discos. We've played to over 200,000 unchurched people in places such as these, and can count on one hand the number of times it's not been 100% accepted. If you take the gospel to people in an open way, so that folk know exactly what you stand for, then everyone is happy. But if you hide that light under a bushel, then people don't really know what's going on and they will think that you're getting at them in an underhand way. Which you probably are.

Probably what we don't realize is that the world *wants* to know about Jesus! And Jesus said that whether they want to hear about the kingdom of God or not, it's our duty to tell them! People are sick of 'normality': they want something real and exciting, because it's a fact that all life consists of for most people is . . . going to work to earn some money to buy some food to give themselves the energy to get up and go to work to earn some money to buy some food etc. etc. Why waste time writing songs about life and how boring it is, if you have the *key* to life?

So summing up the question 'Shouldn't I know what's going on in the secular world?' My answer is . . . of course you should! It's vital that you can have an ordinary conversation with your neighbour, because by winning his friendship you also win his confidence, and you are then in a good position to tell him of what Jesus has done for you and what he can do for him! And if you feel the Lord asking you to go into the world with the gospel, then go! But get your priorities absolutely right, decide whether you are still on milk or not, and make up your mind whether you are strong enough to stand up against a world that will do a good job of trying to lure you back into it.

...I find the Bible hard to read

There are parts of the Bible that *everyone* finds hard to read, so you're not on your own! Remember though, the Bible isn't a glorified story book. It's much, much more. There's an awful lot of history attached to the Bible, and we all know how hard history books were to digest in school! Dates, names and places, piles upon piles of them. Did you ever read your history book straight through from cover to cover? So why try and do it with the Bible! It's much too rich a book to swallow in one gulp. The pattern of the Bible too is very intricate, so that you get references telling you to turn back six chapters to re-read a verse in connection with the bit you're reading now. And of course that verse six chapters back will give you another reference to nine books further on, etc, etc. Confusing? Of course! But what these references are trying to say is, 'Look! What you're reading was prophesied back in the Old Testament years ago, and that prophecy was still being talked about hundreds of years later, after it actually happened!' Past, present and future; all woven very neatly together with not a flaw in sight. The Bible's an astonishing book, but we need to find our own best way of reading it. Here are a few suggestions, most of which I've tried myself and found very helpful.

There are scores of different versions of the Bible, in a variety of shapes and colours, and I think it's important to get the one that is just right for you. Years ago, a Christian did not feel complete without a massive leather-bound Thompson chain-reference Bible tucked under his arm—a terrifying sight for your average man in the street to come up against, especially if the Christian had decided it was your day to get saved! I'm not knocking big Bibles, I think they're great. But they're of more use for studying at home. If you are the type of person that constantly carries a Bible in a pocket or a bag, then obviously the smaller the better, especially if you're going to read it on the train or bus. After all, using a big one for this purpose is like wearing a T-shirt with 'Look at me, aren't I holy?' written on it. Bibles aren't black any more, they come in a variety of bright colours and tasteful designs. Personally I love the ones with the mock-denim covers that go so easily with my jeans and look so nice when witnessing to the denim generation. I find more folk pick up my Bible to scan through if the book is attractive to look at. Maybe you think it's silly to waste time on choosing the right-looking Bible, but you have got to live with it, and being 'comfortable' with your Bible is a good thing. Have you ever been handed someone else's and been asked to find a verse? Now, if it had been your own faithful Bible, you would have found that verse in seconds, but in someone else's it's a different story! Their book is bigger/smaller than yours, it's set out differently and the wrong pages are worn. So it is important to get a Bible and stick to it!

Also of course the inside is pretty important too. When looking at new versions, I always look up a few of my favourite verses and see how they have been phrased. In a Bible shop you can have fun comparing all the different ways there are of saying the same thing! Some are paraphrased versions, and some are more literal translations. This means that in a paraphrased Bible, the writer has taken maybe a verse or a passage and summarized it in his own words, whereas a more literal translation is one where the writer has translated very nearly word for word into modern English. Both are extremely useful, the paraphrase being especially helpful for getting a clear picture of what is going on in that particular chapter.

Once you have chosen your life-long companion, your next move is how to read it effectively, I think there are several good ways. In the Bible bookshop where you purchased your version, they will have reading plans. These are little mapped-out timetables covering the whole of the Bible, and by reading so much a day, you will have read the whole Bible in a year, or two years, depending on the plan. That is a good idea if you want to put yourself through a crash course to get a rough picture of the Bible as a whole, but it usually entails reading five or six chapters a day, and I don't think you can really take it all in, unless you have a particularly studious mind. Most people read a chapter from the Old, a chapter from the New and a psalm. I like this particular plan, because if you start at Genesis 1, Matthew 1 and Psalm 1, you will gradually work your way through the book in your own time, and you'll get a lot out of it. Another good thing to do is to mark and underline things. In my present Bible, each time I read a chapter I put a tick by it. In this way I can check myself against reading and re-reading my favourite books, and make sure I do the others as well. Underlining a verse that the Lord gave you is a great help, especially if you have enough room to write the day by it, or a brief explanation as to why he gave it to you.

Not only will it always remind you how the Lord helped you out, but you will always be able to find that verse in a hurry.

If you are the artistic type, then try gathering together some soft pencil shades and lightly colouring over some helpful verses, e.g. blue for verses inspiring faith, green for promises of God, etc. All the time you are doing these things you are storing up a knowledge of God's word—without even realizing you're doing it! No doubt now that I've given you a few ideas, you will be coming up with a lot more of your own!

One crazy day, John (my husband) and I thought of a new way to bring real life into the letters in the New Testament. We chose a chapter and decided to pretend that it had come from a modern-day Paul to us personally. Yes, we did the whole thing: I ran outside and posted a small Bible through our letter box, and then a few minutes later I came into the house with 'Hi John, I'm home. Anything good in the mail today?' John replied, 'I'm glad you're back. I think we've got a letter from Paul!' This conversation went on for a while until we actually got round to reading the letter. By the time we read it, we were really believing that this was a letter for *us*, and we got a tremendous amount of enjoyment—not to mention teaching—from this somewhat weird way of reading the Bible.

Yet another helpful aid, if you have a room of your own, is to read aloud. Not only does it help you to get used to your own voice (training for prayer meetings!) but it also helps you remember what you've read!

As I was saying earlier, you can't plough through a book like the Bible. I can read a paperback novel very quickly; I'm often told that I *devour* books rather than read them. Before now, I've read a paperback while travelling from the Midlands to Lancashire in our bumpy van! But I don't think the Lord intended us to use the Bible like that. There's so much in it that it can take a long time just to let one verse worm its way into your mind. Everything in the Bible is inspired by the Holy Spirit and is there for the purpose of showing the real Jesus and for bringing us closer to him. The more you read the Bible, the closer you will get to Jesus, as the Holy Spirit inspires you and draws you deeper into the things of God. This is when the Bible starts to really live. If you open the book with the attitude 'I really want to know God' then the Bible will become your greatest inspiration.

And talking of different versions (as we were earlier on . . .), how about writing your own? No, hold on, I wasn't really meaning that you should attempt to re-write the whole Bible. But I have found that occasionally re-writing a chapter is a great way to have a Bible study without realizing you're having one! It's absolutely amazing how much of the Bible we read without really understanding what we've read! Writing it in your own way ensures that you've understood what you've read, and it's tremendous fun if you get together with a few friends and write it between you. One word of warning, though. Re-writing can become compulsive, like cryptic crosswords, you just can't put it down. Also, don't forget to arm yourself with at least a Bible dictionary and an ordinary dictionary. Concordances are cheating a bit, but helpful to check with afterwards.

Reading your Bible, then, is helpful for guidance in your Christian life, for inspiration in prayer, and it can be fun as well. I firmly believe that the Lord laughs along with us as well as sharing our burdens, and because of this we share our Bible-reading time with him and he shows us the things that are important for our lives at the time. So the whole thing builds up our relationship with God.

That's why we have a Bible. It wasn't sent so that you would have to slave away studying as part of being saved. John says it in John 20:31 – 'These have been written that you may believe that Jesus is the Messiah, the Son of God, and that through this faith you may have life in his name.'

Never forget that Jesus came to give us *life* in all its fullness, and the last thing he wants is for Christianity to be a drag, a set of rules. The Lord gave you a mind, an imagination, so get it working and start discovering the tremendous things that God's word is dying to say to you!

...Praying's hard too!

'Dear Lord, thank you for today, it was great. Thanks for helping me talk to that girl. . . . I wonder what happened after, she probably went home and told her mum. Anyway, thanks for that, Lord. Oh, we've got exams tomorrow Lord, I bet I've learnt all the wrong things. That reminds me, I've got to get a new pen otherwise my writing will be *so* bad. Sorry, Lord, what was I saying? Ah yes, bless my exam efforts tomorrow, Lord. Amen.'

Ever prayed like that? Horrible, isn't it? You really want to talk to the Lord, but somehow you stray off the point, start thinking to yourself and not doing any constructive praying at all. Okay, let's do some basic praying. There are a few ways of doing this. Probably one of the most helpful and easiest to remember is the ACTS system.

The letter A stands for Adoration. Spend time at

the beginning of your prayer just praising the Lord. Think of the world he created; try to get an idea of the 'immenseness' of God, the magnificence of the universe and the beauty of life itself. When you get sufficiently in awe, you will find it easy to praise God.

C stands for confession. You'll find it easier to talk with the Lord once you've got things off your chest. It's a fact that confession is good for your soul, and the Bible tells you to do it, in 1 John 1:9. (See the chapter on 'I can't stand Jenny'.) Once you've had a time of telling Jesus everything—yes, everything—then you will feel ready for T.

T stands for thanksgiving. There is no way you can ever thank the Lord enough for all the things he's done for you!

And S is for supplication. That is, prayer for other people. Prayer requests and the like, the thing you normally do first, the great long shopping list! It's good to pray for other people and to let God know your requests, but it's also good to spend time just *with* the Lord! There's a famous verse in the Bible (Matthew 6:33 AV) which says, 'Seek ye first the kingdom of God, and his righteousness; and all these things shall be added unto you.' In other words, if you are doing God's will, then the Lord is going to look after your needs. Most of the Bible promises have an 'if' in them; most of them say things like 'If you stay close to me, I'll stay close to you.' And one of the best ways of keeping close to Jesus is praying.

Answers to prayer often seem to be a problem to folk. People say, 'I never see answers to prayer, they always happen to other people.' Well, maybe you're not asking for outstanding things! Or maybe you're asking for the wrong things! We limit God something terrible. . . . We don't bother to pray for the impossible, because *we* think the situation is impossible! How can we prove that God can do the impossible unless we give him a chance to prove it? And in saying that, I don't mean that we should tempt the Lord by yelling out 'Prove it!' The devil tried that, and the Lord rebuked him with scriptures. Just when *we* can't see how on earth the Lord is going to solve a particular problem, we decide it is *above* praying for! But that's why God is God! Because he specializes in things thought to be impossible. . . .

Listen to this testimony about our guitarist, Chuck.

When Chuck was fifteen, he had virtually given up being a Christian. He hadn't gone wild or anything, but he wasn't getting anything out of his Christian life. He wasn't seeing Jesus working in his everyday life. Then, completely out of the blue, a series of events happened which completely changed his view about a living God. One Christmas Eve, Chuck's dad collapsed. Actually, the family weren't too worried: his dad often collapsed if he was about to have an attack of the flu. But when the morning came, there was no sign of any kind of cold, and so the doctor was called in. The doctor was mystified, and suggested a few days in hospital for a series of tests. After the hospital tests they were still not sure, but it seemed as if the illness was much more serious than first suspected. In fact, they thought that Chuck's dad had either a foreign virus, or a tumour on the brain. The only way they could find out more was to fly his dad from Guernsey, where they were living, to England.

By this time, his dad was worse, and things were looking pretty bad. I'll let Chuck take up a bit of the story. 'By the time they took my dad to England, he looked deathly, and though they said they were taking him away, not a lot was said about him ever coming back again.'

So Chuck decided he should think about leaving school to earn a wage to help his mum. But meanwhile he was aware that the local church were praying a lot for his dad. 'I wasn't ungrateful, but I thought, well, if that's their way of helping—fine, but I'll do the sensible thing, and get myself a job. I didn't hold much with the power of prayer.'

When his dad finally got to England, the doctors there carried out a mass of tests, and when the results came through . . . there was nothing wrong. Nothing at all. And six weeks later Chuck's dad was back at work. 'I couldn't really understand it, but I did wonder if it had anything to do with these 'weirdo Christians' that had been praying for my dad, but I pushed the thought to the back of my mind.'

But that was not the end, because shortly afterwards, Chuck landed in hospital himself! He was playing a game of football for the school, when the ball came up and caught him in the face. He was stunned for a minute and then his right eye started to give him considerable pain. The referee took no notice of Chuck lying on the ground, as he knew him to be quite a joker and thought he was just fooling around. But when Chuck failed to get up after several minutes, the ref came over to check the injury. 'The referee asked me if my eye was usually bloodshot, and then told me that the bottom third was completely red! He tried to make me count his fingers by holding up his hand, but I couldn't even see his *hand*, let alone his fingers!'

Chuck was taken to hospital where they found he had a burst blood vessel at the back of his eye. The doctor told him that an operation would be necessary as there was no way the blood could clear up by itself. 'I was scared. I'm allergic to pain and I was terrified at the thought of an operation!'

The next day, he had a visit from my husband John. (John was the minister of the church that Chuck had once used to go to.) It was a rather strange meeting, as Chuck had both his eyes bandaged. 'I'd only met John once before, and then I'd bid him a hurried hello and disappeared!'

Chuck was surprised to find that ministers could have ordinary conversations! So they chatted about football for a while, and then, when it was time for John to go, he asked if Chuck would mind if he prayed for him. 'I didn't really see what good it would do, but I didn't want to hurt his feelings, so I said "Go ahead."' John prayed for the healing of Chuck's eye, and then he left. 'A few minutes later, my eye started to really hurt, and I remember thinking, "Huh! fat lot of good *that* prayer did! I feel worse now than before he prayed for me!"'

But that afternoon the surgeon came to see him and checked his eye. 'It's amazing!' the doctor said, 'but your eye is clearing up by itself!' Then he explained to Chuck what had actually happened.

When the football had hit the eye, it had caused a blood vessel to burst, and the only way to stop the flow was to make Chuck sit up all night to give the blood a chance to dry. Once the blood had dried, the only way to remove it was by an operation involving taking his eye out and removing the dried blood from the back of it. But in this case, the blood had removed itself! 'You're a lucky bloke' smiled the doctor. However, Chuck knew different. He realized that prayer was the only way that his eye had been healed, and that at the moment when his eye had started to give him pain, the blood was in fact being removed . . . straight after John's prayer!

The fact that God had cared for Chuck, when Chuck wasn't that interested in God, was a big enough thing to make him turn round and devote his life to Jesus.

Prayer can do strange things. In one way, prayer healed the impossible, but looking at it the other way, it also gained a dedicated Christian. The prayer that John had prayed wasn't a fancy one, or long and drawn out; it was just a simple prayer, trusting God to do what normally couldn't be done.

We must remember too that when God answers prayer, it's not always 'Yes' that he says. There's also a 'No' or a 'Wait', and we must be prepared to accept God's decision, even though it may sound strange to us at the time. If you look back on some of the things you've prayed about, you can probably see now why God didn't answer in the way you wanted him to at the time. The Lord knows our future, he knows what's good for us, the same way as your own father knows what's good for you. When you're little, you want sweets, sweets and more sweets, but your dad knows what'll happen if he lets you devour the amount of chocolate that you have your eye on! Maybe he would say to you, 'You know, your eyes are bigger than your stomach!' And he would be right! When we're young we think we can eat every bit of chocolate in the world, but our stomach knows different! And if we go ahead anyway, we soon find out who was right and who was wrong! And so it is with your heavenly father. We may not see it, but he always knows best.

Summing up on praying, we have to turn again to see what Jesus had to say. He said that when we pray, there's a very good pattern we should follow, and if we pray about all these things, then we're not doing badly: 'Our Father, which art in heaven, hallowed be thy name. Thy kingdom come. Thy will be done on earth as it is in heaven. Give us this day our daily bread, and forgive us our trespasses as we forgive them that trespass against us; and lead us not into temptation, but deliver us from evil. For thine is the kingdom, the power and the glory, for ever and ever. Amen.'

...I'm in love with my schoolteacher

'And as she looked up from her drink, their eyes met across the crowded room, and nothing needed to be said. . . .'

Have you ever sighed and thought how wonderful it would be to fall in love like that? To just know in your heart exactly how you felt, and that he or she felt exactly the same way too! Now I know you've heard a lot of people tell you it's all rubbish and it doesn't happen like that. Well, I'm here to tell you different!

I very much hope that one day you will meet the one and only person in the world that you would gladly share the rest of your life with.

Unfortunately there is a 99% chance it will not be your schoolteacher, or anyone else that you look up to in awe and admiration. Reason? Because love is a two-way thing, and however much you may desperately adore someone, it will never come to anything tremendous unless that person feels exactly the same way as you do. And that can be terribly sad and heartbreaking at the time; which somehow only seems to make you want that person more. It's a fact that anything out of reach is far more attractive at that distance. It has mystery and romance attached to it simply because you can't have it.

But how many times have you managed to grasp the mystery only to be desperately disappointed?

Remember someone who never used even to glance your way, and then on that glorious day he/she spoke to you and turned out to have a lisp and bad breath and a nauseating way of looking at you?

I know when I started working with pop stars at the grand old age of 17, I was always amazed how ordinary they were. I always expected them to be so much the 'big star'. But they were always 'gasping for a cuppa' just like everyone else. They got back-ache, tooth-ache and had B.O. like the rest of the world. It's a bit of a shake-up at the time, but it's a shake-up we all need now and then.

Fantasy and reality are, as a rule, a few miles apart, and while there is no harm in day-dreaming, it's just as well to be reminded of the truth. By that I don't mean that just because your dream girl or fella is in the Olivia Newton John/John Travolta bracket, you will automatically end up with someone at the other end of the scale. I sincerely hope you meet up with his or her equivalent, *but* it's a 99.9% chance that it won't be your actual star!

So how do you know when it's real?

Well, first of all, I'm going to take it that you are a Christian, saved by the cross of Jesus, and that you believe in his plan for your life. Therefore whether you like it or not Jesus is in control of your love-life, because you are his child. That means, forget non-Christians when it comes to being serious about your partner. God has a far more preferable match for you! So if your partner is not a Christian, you can guarantee he's not the ultimate one for you. He may be everything you ever dreamed of, but that's only because you haven't met the one that the Lord has waiting for you. Don't fall into the trap of 'Well, after we're married it'll be different,' because if it's already a worrying undercurrent now, it can only worsen once you are living so close together. And of course, your other half is thinking, 'She'll forget all about church once we're settled down,' so you're both walking into a life-time of the same old stubborn argument. Can you really imagine that God wants that for you? God wants you to have the very best there is. You're his child and he wants to see you perfectly matched, even more than your own doting earthly parents do! Looking on the negative side, then, if it's you and a non-Christian, then it's not 100% real.

Childhood sweethearts can also be a bit of a disaster. If you grow up for years and years with the same date, you could well get too comfy to move around and see what others are like. People often drift into a marriage this way—I know, as I almost did it myself. I'll always be grateful to a certain member of a pop group for asking me this question: 'Why are you engaged to someone you don't love?' It was a shattering blow to realize that other people could see that we were just drifting along aimlessly. Sometimes it takes someone else to confront you like that, to wake you up. So if you are drifting, it's not real either.

This is another strange factor. As I said earlier, I believe you can fall in love at first sight; I believe also that you can grow to love someone over a period of time. I wouldn't feel happy about someone marrying in the hope that love would eventually arrive. I've been married seven years, which isn't all that long to be handing out advice (apart from a few things). I've not come across more than a handful of marriages that are as happy and full as ours. A lot of couples, after one or two years of marriage, have become staid and irritable—and here I include Christian marriages!

One week in April 1972, John and I met. John was the guest preacher at our church, and I was up in the pulpit giving a testimony. We went out together, and at the end of the first week, John asked me to marry him. *Nothing* was more natural and right than to say yes. We both absolutely knew that it was right; there was no doubt in either of our minds that we were in love and that the Lord had brought us together.

So one way to know if it's the real thing is if you are 100% sure of not only your love for that special person, but of his/her love for you! It's no good you trying to carry enough love for two people, because you will only manage that for a while and then it will be just too much to cope with. Falling in love can happen in thousands of different ways, from bumping into someone in the street, to being introduced to your best friend's girl! But just be sure that you *are* sure before you make any kind of commitment to each other.

I don't want to turn this chapter into a sex talk, but I think it's worth mentioning that for a Christian, sex comes after marriage—every time—no exceptions! That's a Bible-based fact, and maybe you think that your problem is totally different. But be sure that the Lord won't bless it. In the few Christian 'problem pages' that I've come across, the problems are very much the same. They all have a differently disguised wrapper on them, but they all boil down to 'Can I have sex before marriage?' And the answer is no. I know that you know that the answer is no, but you're always hoping that if you read enough Christian material, you'll get the go-ahead. Sorry pal, I don't think you'll ever find a scripture that tells you to go ahead and sin!

Really the majority of the subjects in this book are plain common sense, but somehow we all need the reassurance that what we think is right, is right! And when it comes to marriage, then it has to be right! Marriage is the second most important decision you will ever have to make. The first most important decision is where you are going to spend eternity!

When girls are just coming up to leaving age at school, there is a competition that's played in about every school in the world, and that's the race to see who can get engaged first, or even married! There's a gap between leaving school and getting married, and that gap should be filled with you enjoying your freedom from responsibility, buying loads of crazy clothes and records, flitting from job to job and generally having fun. Maybe that sounds flippant, but for a girl, a job is not usually for life (unless you're particularly career-minded), which is why a lot of adverts for jobs in banks and such like include a special scheme for girls who will only be staying for a few years until they get married.

But when you're at school, there's this special something about setting up house and having babies, putting flowers in your own front garden and walking the dog. And the more you talk about it, the more you want it, and before you know it, you are trying to beat all your friends in the race to find the first available fella and show off the ring! I saw an enormous amount of my school friends get engaged and married within a few years of leaving school at the age of sixteen. Unhappily, I've seen a few of them since, and they look exactly the same as when they left school. They are wearing the same clothes, same hair-styles, but their faces are worn and plain, and they exist to drag unwanted kids around the shops and shout at them. They completely missed out on those years of fun, and seemingly missed out on the right match too.

And what of the guys? Well, I guess there's something ultra-masculine about being a husband, and of course more so, being a father.

That's one up on your mates, isn't it? But that's about all it is, because there are few kids who leave school with such good jobs that they can support a wife and children, let alone a massive mortgage! Most fellas have some kind of career in mind, and careers usually mean starting at the bottom and working your way up to the top. And starting at the bottom means poor wages. Clerk to Managing Director is a long hard climb, but well worth it in the end, whereas the kind of job that sees money straight away is usually the type of job where you sit at a bench and screw a nut on to a bolt, and then the bolt moves up on the conveyor belt and you start all over again with the next nut and bolt. This motion goes on until the whistle blows and it's time to go home. . . . The money's good—so's the overtime, but the job itself will drive you crazy! And you will have to do that every day, maybe for the rest of your life, because you now have no experience in any other form of work.

So from that point of view, it's a shame to get married at school-leaving age. Have a look around you, and see how many married couples you know who have married that early, and then put yourself in their place. I said earlier, that I am all for romance and love at first sight, but it's best not to get it muddled up with fantasy. In fact, fantasy is fast becoming a popular word. In films and TV people often talk about their real lives and their fantasy lives, and in some cases the fantasy is more real than the real! Fantasy is you at school, dreaming of making some exotic dish for your husband's tea, and then settling down by the fireside to dream away the rest of the evening. Reality is you not having the slightest idea how to cook a *snack* let alone an exotic dish, and your husband coming in from his day of nuts and bolts, and not caring for anything but his armchair by the fire and *Match of the Day*.

To find romance in everyday living like that, your love has to be real. So once again, I would suggest that you make very sure that your partner is *the* one for you, the one that the Lord has chosen for you. Then the hearts and flowers side of things will be very real, and not just the things you dreamed of while sitting at your desk, carving initials in the wood with your compasses.

...I don't 'feel led' very often

There are many things that go under the guise of 'feeling led' and most of them are silly and easy to spot, but a few are a bit more serious.

Noah, for instance, was very much led by God to build a hideous boat in the middle of nowhere and fill it with animals, while all he had to go on was that God had told him it was going to rain. The Bible says that Noah was a godly man, and I think that being godly had a lot to do with Noah feeling led. Noah was very close to God and had a good 'servant-master' relationship with him, and because of this God could trust Noah to obey him.

But when it comes to us, we aren't always available when the Lord says 'move'. In fact, most of the time, we just plain don't hear him, either because we don't want to, or because we're not close enough to him.

But hang on, let's concentrate first on the guises—those times when people use 'I feel led' as an excuse to do something they've always wanted to do.

Too many times I've heard people say, 'The Lord has given me a good voice and I'd like to sing this song to his glory!' when what they really mean is, 'Listen to me, I've got a great voice and I'm going to sing about God!' Or worse still they say, 'I was lying in bed one night praying and God gave me the words and music to this song, so although I wrote it down, really it was the Lord that gave me the song. In fact I have written all my own songs with God to guide me.' This is just puffed-up pride bursting to get out! Now, the terrible thing about this kind of 'leading' is that nine times out of ten the songs are atrocious! The Lord, who gave us music, would never have written such rubbish! It's a real shame to blame the Lord for our failings, and such a bad witness to kids that aren't saved who have had to suffer the songs in question.

It's true that if you step out in faith, the chances are that you will be laughed at, as Noah was, and like Noah you will have to stick your neck out. But God is not liable to lead you specifically every day. When you put your faith in God to save you, he automatically took over your life. But he didn't take your life away—he gave it back to you, on loan if you like. The Lord owns you now, and if he needs you to do anything special, he'll tell you in no uncertain terms. Meanwhile he expects you to have enough common sense to deal with living. A lot of people feel they have to ask the Lord's advice on what to have for dinner, whether to catch a bus or train, and so on, into every minor detail.

Let me tell you of someone I knew. If he were giving out tracts in the street and one dropped on the floor, he would say, 'No, I won't pick it up. The Lord wants it on the pavement, perhaps someone is going to come along and pick it up, read it and get saved!' Tragic really, when you think that all morning he has been giving out tracts and the vast majority looked at the tract and threw it on the pavement anyway. This guy spent so long 'being led' on the way to work that he eventually got the sack from his job because he was never there on time.

Another good trick is to get halfway to work and feel that the Lord doesn't want you to go that particular day. This is commonly known as shirking. I've met numerous Christians, sad to say, who have dolefully looked up at me and said, 'I really tried to get on that train, but obviously God didn't want me to.' Pretty ironic, then, that the rest of the day was spent listening to records under the headphones of a certain record shop that I worked in.

So what is feeling led? When is God going to make you stand in a train-ticket queue with no money so that someone can come up at the last minute and issue you with the exact amount? As I said, it *can* happen, but not every day, and it only happened to Abraham and other Bible heroes a handful of times. Feeling led isn't usually accompanied by apathy, a feeling of 'Oh well, I don't fancy doing that so God obviously doesn't want me to do it.' It's more often the other way round. God says, 'Do this,' and you say, 'Oh no, Lord, *anything* but that!' Take for example a lady I know who was praying in the Communion service. She suddenly felt an overwhelming desire to pray for a friend of hers who was a missionary. She felt the Lord say to her, 'Go to the Communion table and plead the blood for your friend.' But the lady thought, 'I can't—I can't just rush out to the front in the middle of a service and kneel and plead at the Communion table!' But the feeling of pressure from the Lord got stronger and stronger, and in the end she stood up and prayed aloud, pleading the blood for her friend. But still she didn't go to the table. After the service, she left feeling discouraged because she had felt led by the Lord and had not obeyed. Later in the week she heard that her friend had died at the hands of natives at the same time on Sunday as the Lord was leading her to pray. Tragic—yes. But neither you nor I would have been much different, because when God is leading you, it isn't easy. As I said, it has nothing to do with sloppiness or 'not feeling like it'; it's usually a difficult thing to do.

I don't think there's any real pattern as to how the Lord leads people. Sometimes God speaks in a very real voice, sometimes he writes on the wall, sometimes we just have a feeling. But most times we don't realize that the Lord has led us until we look back on the occasion. The silly thing is that, when God does very plainly ask us to do something, we don't take any notice anyway. 'You are weighed in the balance and found wanting,' was the slogan that the Lord wrote on a wall in the house of a chap named Belshazzar. Boy, was Belshazzar terrified! The Bible even refers to the fact that his knees were knocking together, he was so frightened. So what did he do about it? Nothing! Good old Christian nothing! If Belshazzar did nothing about God's totally obvious prompting, then why do you think *you'd* be any different?

When the Lord started calling our group Dunamis away to the mainland from Guernsey, we ignored what he was trying to tell us for ages. We started our group in the church as an attempt to liven up our stunningly average Sunday-night meetings.

I don't know if you've ever tried to form a group, but it's not quite as easy as it sounds. When we first started to rehearse, we were diabolical. Then we gradually progressed to pathetic, and when we were just plain 'bad' we tried it out on the church! Well, you know what churches are . . . they loved it! They so admired the fact that young Christians were actually doing something for a change that they thought we were wonderful! Of course we were not wonderful at all, but our egos were boosted enough for us to have a go at another song. Before a few months were out, we were being asked to sing in lots of different churches all over the island of Guernsey. This was the first time that we wondered if God was trying to tell us something . . . and of course we ignored the feeling completely and carried on our own sweet way.

But not long afterwards, we were asked to go to the island of Alderney to take a three-day campaign. Alderney is an island about the size of an average postage stamp (okay, so that's a slight exaggeration) and it holds around 1800 people. There are roughly 140 teenagers over there, and I just can't imagine what it must be like living in such a small place and seeing the same faces every day of your life, but that's where we were heading.

Publicity was a bit awkward. Can you imagine printing up a load of leaflets and handing them out to the same half-a-dozen people as they walked up and down the only main road? No, this needed a little bit more planning than that. However, a Salvation Army officer came to our rescue by offering this unique solution: 'How about coming on a pub crawl with me? Every Saturday I go round the pubs selling my *War Cry* so why don't you come with me? You could sing a song and then tell everyone where the crusade is being held.'

Well, it was different! But that is exactly what we did. And here is where the Lord had his second chat with us about the group, because as we went from pub to pub singing the gospel to the local people, we had some startling reactions. One man said to us, 'If only you had been doing this when I was searching for God, when I needed someone to talk to, I would have come with you . . . but now I feel it's too late.' We hastily told him it was never too late to get right with God, but he felt that his big moment had passed. Another guy came up to us and said, 'This is where you Christians should be! You should be in here telling us about Jesus, not stuck in your churches! What's the use of putting up a poster outside a church saying 'Welcome'. I mean, who's going to come in to a church where they don't know anybody? No, *this* is where you Christians should be!' Yet another man came up to us while we were singing in a cabaret on the island, and said, 'I'm a retired inspector from Scotland Yard, and when I left England I felt that there was no hope for those young kids back there on the mainland. But if there's going to be people like you going around public places and telling everyone about the gospel, then I think there is still hope for England!'

Perhaps you can see that the Lord was obviously speaking to us, but we couldn't! We just thought to ourselves, 'How strange, maybe the Lord's trying to tell us something!' When you look back on the times when the Lord has led you along a certain path, you can see it quite clearly for yourself, but at the time the whole thing is so misty.

On coming back to Guernsey after a successful time in Alderney, where we had seen many kids coming to Jesus, we found ourselves faced with yet another crazy offer to sing. This time it was for a banker! Paul (affectionately known as Chuck), our guitarist, was working in a bank at the time and they decided to have a party-cum-get-together for no real reason. So they hired a hotel bar and started making arrangements for the party to go with a swing. Strangely enough, *that* was when they said to Chuck, 'How about your group coming to sing for us?' Chuck tried to explain that we were purely a gospel group and that we only sang songs about Jesus, and how he couldn't see it going down at a party where everyone was intent on getting sloshed and generally merry. Unfortunately (so we thought) the majority of employees thought it was a great idea, and so with trembling knees and not much faith, Chuck agreed for us to do it. I suppose somewhere in the back of our minds was the thought that we had actually already sung in pubs with a good reaction, but whether it would work for a whole evening was rather a different matter.

The hotel thing was a great success. Everyone enjoyed our music and quite a few even got into the words. The amazing thing was the number of people who wanted to sit around and chat after the performance. They wanted to know where our church was, why we believed in Jesus, and why we were not singing for money and only about God. It was sort of like counselling people in a coffee bar situation where they are not sure whether they want to accept Jesus or not. When we came home, we were pretty quiet. The Lord was beginning to speak in a louder voice and it was getting difficult to ignore. We did get round to chatting about the fact that the Lord seemed to be using us in very outreachy sorts of places, and we did actually wonder if perhaps he was leading us up to something. I believe that at this point every member of the group knew that the Lord wanted to call us out of a church ministry and into the world . . . but not one of us was going to suggest it, in case anyone else agreed! It was a frightening but exciting time for all of us.

The crunch came on the day we got the letter. In our particular denomination, all the ministers get a sort of circular letter that tells you who's died, who's got married, and all the general gossip. Well, in this particular letter, there was a very insignificant paragraph that had words to this effect: 'We are looking for a team of young people to give up a year of their lives to help out in Christian youth work. We are especially looking for singers, guitarists and people who can give a good testimony. If you have any such folk in your church who would like to put their names forward, please get in touch with us!'

I guess the thing that came across in that paragraph more than anything was that there was no mention of a minister to lead this 'team'. Therefore they had already asked a minister to lead this team, and as our group was headed by John who was in fact a minister there was no point in offering our services. And yet, somehow we knew we should. Christian youth work didn't sound all that appealing, but we felt that if we could share our vision with our headquarters, maybe they would allow us to go ahead and start evangelizing England! We had almost come to the place now where we were acknowledging the fact that the Lord was sending us out into the world with his gospel! So why not phone the main man and offer the group to him? You know what it's like when you get excited about something. We sat around rehearsing what John would say to him, and we wrote down everything we could think of that might help sway his mind and let us go! Anyway, when we phoned him . . . he wasn't in! They never are, are they? However, later the next day, when everyone was at work and Mutley (our dog) had taken John over the park, the phone rang. I answered it, and of course it was the man about the letter. I tried hard to fob him off with 'Oh so sorry, John's out at the moment. Could you phone back?' But he wasn't going to be put off quite that easily, so he said, 'Can't you tell me what it was about?' He couldn't really have asked a worse person, because by now I was in a state of advanced panic as I realized that our whole chance of going to England was being piled on my shoulders, and I had to make a jolly good job of this!

I can vaguely remember saying something like 'Ah! well you see we got your letter but probably you didn't want a minister anyway, but we do sing harmonies and we're quite good, well not bad, but the letter said about a team and we felt that, well it was just an idea and it doesn't really matter, we just thought we'd apply anyway. . . .'

I still can't understand *how* he interpreted that mess, but at the end of it all, he replied, 'This is strange. I was just sitting here praying to the Lord and saying, 'Lord, I'm sure you want this team, so how come I've not had any satisfactory replies?' Then I glanced down and saw a message to phone John, and you have just offered a complete team! I think it's tremendous. Yes, you can do it. When do you want to start?'

I mean, can the Lord speak any clearer than that? He had not only told us to go out, but he had provided a way for us to start! We were absolutely elated because the Lord had made it so clear that we were about to do the right thing. All we needed now was the faith to step out into completely unknown circumstances. The next chapter will deal with 'active faith', so if you want to know how we got on—please keep going!

...I have no faith

It is a strange thing that we are saved by faith. The day you asked Jesus to come into your life, you put all your faith and trust in him to save you from eternal punishment. You believed that God had a plan for your life that included sending his only son Jesus Christ to die instead of you. At least, I hope that you are sure of your salvation.

Perhaps we could spend just a few minutes on checking out what 'being saved' is all about, as it could be that you are still unsure. God created the world, right? When he put you and I on to that world he gave us a choice: we could either believe in him, or reject him. He didn't want you to be a robot, otherwise he would have said, 'Okay, everybody believe in me, full stop.' But he didn't do that, because he is not that kind of God, so he gave you a choice. God had a plan to help you with that choice, and this was it. He planned an ultimate sacrifice. To help you understand what sacrifice is all about, I'll explain. . . .

In the days of the Old Testament, they had what was known as the Day of Atonement. This was a very solemn day, because on that day the sins of the nation were symbolically taken away. The high priest would go into the Temple and take with him an innocent animal. Then he would sacrifice the animal, and take some of its blood into a place known as the 'Holy of Holies'. The 'Holy of Holies' was a very sacred compartment in the depth of the Temple where only the high priest was allowed to go. In this room was a box, and in the box were the ten commandments (which man had broken), Aaron's rod, symbolizing authority (which man did not want) and some manna (man didn't want the food that God provided, he wanted meat instead). So the objects in the box represented man's sin against God. Over the box were two cherubim which represented God looking down on man's sin. The blood of the animal would cover the box, and while the blood was there, God could not see man's sins: he could only see the blood.

Unhappily, the sacrifice of an innocent animal was not enough to warrant more than a day's forgiveness, because at the end of that day the priest would come out of the Temple and the people would have to wait another year before their sins were dealt with again.

So God had to find a way of making that sacrifice permanent, and the only way that pure sacrifice could be made was for his son Jesus to offer himself. That's why the Bible says that God gave us his only son (John 3:16). When Jesus died his blood covered our sins and God could not see anything but the blood of Jesus. But then Jesus rose from the dead and went to reign in heaven. And he's still there! That means that as long as Jesus is with God, your sins are covered and you are forgiven . . . *if* you have the faith to believe that Jesus died for you! Here's a couple of verses from Galatians 2 which will really help you, especially if you learn them parrot fashion!

'I have been crucified with Christ and I no longer live, but Christ lives in me. The life I live in the body, I live by *faith in the Son of God, who loved me and gave himself for me.* I do not set aside the grace of God, for if righteousness could be gained through the law [the Holy of Holies ritual], Christ died for nothing!' (Galatians 2:20-21 NIV). So you have been saved by faith, and now that you are a Christian you tend to forget living by faith and go back to the old way of 'trying to be good enough'. People seem to think that they will never have great faith in God because they are always doing things wrong; and yet having faith has got nothing to do with works! You can't work yourself up to the right standard . . . you will never ever be good enough for God to use you as you are. It will always take faith in God to achieve anything worthwhile. Push all the sweat and tears aside and get ready for God to use you. The first thing you need is a very special ability, one that takes an enormous amount of courage. What is it? Avail*ability*! The one thing that people can't bear to do is to strip themselves before the Lord and say, 'Here I am, use me.' That takes a big step of faith, I mean, Jesus might tell you to go to Africa and become a missionary! The chances are he won't want you to go further than your own neighbourhood, but there's always that thought in the back of your mind, that making yourself available is asking for trouble! If you give yourself over to God, then I *know* that he will honour your step of faith and use you. I can guarantee that if you are willing to live by faith then God will take you up on it, for the simple reason that he's desperate for people to use! One word of warning though: don't ever think in terms of becoming a 'super-hero'; you must be genuine in your aim.

When Chuck (our guitarist) was just about to come away with Dunamis, he began to get all these great ideas about touring round the world, being a superstar gospel band, and being nationally acclaimed in his homeland of Guernsey. He became worried, as his initial fire for evangelizing the world was being taken over by a desire to be a hero, and worst of all . . . he was quite enjoying the idea. So he becan to pray: 'Lord, I don't think I'm going for the right reasons. I'm going because I want to be a hero, and if you won't let me be a hero, then I don't want to go!'

Looking back, we can see that this was a gigantic case of nerves at the enormousness of the situation, coupled with a fear of the unknown! Chuck brought this problem to John who prayed with him for a quick answer from the Lord (we were to announce to our church that we were leaving the following day—so it had to be quick!) and prayed that the Lord would show Chuck what to do. The following day nothing had happened, and we sat in the communion service wondering why the Lord hadn't answered John's prayers. Then, all of a sudden, a lady stood up and gave a wonderful prophecy. This women couldn't possibly have known anything about our going away to England, and yet you would swear she had inside knowledge—which I guess in one way she had! I can't remember the prophecy word for word, but it was something like: 'Don't be afraid! Get up and do your exploits for me! I tell you to go, work for me and don't be afraid; you are going to do tremendous exploits in my name!'

Poor Chuck! Not only was the message obviously for him, but the lady in question was standing directly behind him and he could actually feel her breath on the back of his neck! He just cowered in his seat and submitted! When we finally got on board the boat for England, Chuck had no doubts in his mind that he was going for God.

Someone somewhere along the line once said: 'God said it, I believe it, that settles it!' And that really does sum up faith very well. Once we had realized that the Lord was definitely telling us to go over to England, we had to start believing in him for some very big things. To start with, we had to have somewhere to live, so we prayed for a house. Now the thing is, we didn't wait to find out if God was going to supply us with a house *before* we started moving out of our old situation. There's no point in saying to God, 'I believe you are going to give us a house, but just in case you don't, I'll hang on to my job and security until I hear otherwise.' That is not faith. Faith had to say, 'Lord, I have no house to sell, but I've given away my furniture and given in my notice and bought the tickets to England and I believe that you are going to supply us with somewhere to live when we get there!'

There's a verse in Philippians that says, 'I will supply all your needs.' The group have often hung on to that verse like grim death, because to do the kind of outreach we are doing meant giving up everything we owned to buy our musical equipment and the van to travel in. Ah yes, and I forgot to tell you that we don't charge for our ministry, so we have to trust the Lord to supply our daily bread. As you may guess, the churches that we work with will take up an offering for us, or maybe give us something from their funds. But whether they can pay us a wage that we can live on, or whether they can only give us thirty pounds for a week's work between six of us, or even if they just can't pay us at all . . . we still see the need to reach people for Jesus in their area.

So we prayed for a house. We didn't have any money to back us up, but the Lord provided our home through a minister who was in the middle of buying his own house and selling the church manse. The manse had been on sale for eighteen months and no one had bought it. That's what first made the minister think that perhaps God wanted to use the manse for his work. When he heard of our ministry, he came straight out and offered the manse to us, rent-free for a year. Then when the year was up, he would put the manse back on the market and try to sell it again. We were so happy to know that for a year at least, we would have somewhere to live!

Once you step out in faith, it's amazing how soon you have to do it again. I think the Lord likes us to keep exercising our faith so that *next* time we can ask him for something that takes just a little more faith than the last time!

Our house in the Midlands was just that . . . a house. No furniture, no carpets, just a house. It was quite sad thinking back to the furniture we had given away in Guernsey, but there had been no way of bringing it with us in a van that could hardly accommodate six people, suitcases and equipment. So we had to start 'praying in' arm-chairs and things. The idea being that we would try to get one room nice enough to sit in and relax. That's why we started our request with carpets! Alas, our faith was dwindling as we sat on the floorboards in the front room; but gradually, impish grins started spreading across our faces. Here I must let you into a group secret . . . When-ever we can't afford something we need, we go over to our special money box. It's a box where we keep our survival money, that is, money for petrol, insurance stamps, food and boring everyday things like that. This particular day we had exactly £30 to our name and we decided that we would buy a piece of carpet to fit the front room and rely on God to supply the food! When we came back from the carpet store, we had hilarious fun fitting our first piece of carpet. Out came the carving knives, the scissors, the potato peeler, in fact anything that would cut, and we went around trimming the edges. Boy, were we proud of that little piece of carpet! It seemed like our front room had been turned into a palace.

Later that evening there was a knock at the door, and a lady from the local church stood there. She said that she was just popping in to make sure we were all right, and as you can guess, she was dragged into the front room and given a guided tour of the carpet. Finally she got away and went home again. . . . But that night as she was praying she said, 'Lord, I'm so glad that you have made the group so happy over what is to me just a piece of carpet. It's thrilled me, Lord, to see them happy with such a small possession.' All at once, she felt the Lord say to her, 'Well, if you're so happy about it—why don't you carpet the rest of the house?'

Do you know, the next day, that same lady came around to our house and asked us to measure up our three large bedrooms, our middle room and our hallway, and she just went straight out and ordered enough carpet to cover it all! I don't believe for a minute that people go round doing things like that for kicks. I believe the Lord has to prompt you in a mighty way, and we were thrilled to see the Lord using people around us to complete his ministry.

When things like that happen, your faith tends to soar, but it's sad how soon you come down from that 'high'. A few months later, our tour of England was well under way and we started to come up against a few snags. The main one being that every time we came home from three or four weeks on the road, we were so tired that we found we couldn't relax. Therefore, we had to try and find some way of unwinding, and after numerous attempts at playing Scrabble and throwing darts at dartboards and playing records and throwing darts at records and playing dartboards on the record player (only joking, but we did try a lot of silly things!) we finally came up with the ultimate solution! What we needed was a colour TV. . . . No, I know you haven't got one, have you? Have you? Well, we wanted one as well! You see, the idea was that when we came home, we could sit on our well-renowned carpet and be entertained by the box. We had been 'giving out' for weeks and really needed simply to relax. So we got together as a group and prayed in faith for our colour TV. We just told the Lord all about our need to relax, and then left it with him.

Away we went on tour. While we were away we met a couple at a large meeting in London, and brought them home to stay with us for a few days (show them the carpet etc!). When we arrived home, to our horror and amazement, the colour TV was not on the doorstep! We ran inside the house and looked all over the place, but if definitely was not there. This was when doubt began to set in. You see, we all have our different ideas of how God is going to honour prayer, and when he doesn't do it the way we've planned, then we think he isn't going to do it at all!

Never mind, we thought, perhaps we shouldn't have asked for a colour TV, perhaps that wasn't a 'need'—although we really felt it was! Never mind, we thought again, there's always the money box. The money box contained £61. This was supposed to feed us for the week, buy our petrol to the next port of call and do a hundred more mundane things, but once again we decided to blow it. We got quite excited at the thought of going into town and purchasing one of those tiny portable black-and-white TV sets that you can get for around £60. So we took our friends along with us and wandered into the TV shop. Very officially we asked if we could try out a portable TV, and we spent hours jumping up and down getting more excited about it. Meanwhile, the couple that were with us had gone up to the salesman and said, 'Look, leave them while they're happy, but take no notice of that set. We'd like to buy them this colour TV over here.' Once again, the Lord had used other Christians to provide our needs. They told us later that while they were at the London meeting, they felt the Lord telling them to give the group some money. For some reason they held back, and then when they returned to our house, they said they realized how the money could best be used! Anyway, being 'trophies of grace' we gave them our £60 towards the cost of the colour TV and came home very happy. The box was very carefully placed on the carpet, the aerial plugged in and everything in perfect working order. However, when we switched on, the first thing that lit up the screen was an immaculately colourful advert that said, 'Have you got your TV licence?'!

With our £60 spent, we had just one pound with which to buy our licence, and the cost at that time was £21. We took this to the Lord immediately (I wish we took other things to him as fast!) and said, 'Lord, you wouldn't provide us with a TV and then not let us use it, would you?'

Sometimes, I think the Lord's just testing our reaction, for next day in the post was a letter from the organizers of the London meeting, enclosing a cheque for £20, and saying, 'I hope this covers your expenses.' It did! Marvellously well!

When the Lord calls you to live by faith, I don't think he expects you to live a life of poverty! What kind of witness is that? If God is able to bless abundantly, then I can't imagine that he wants us walking around in rags, especially if we are doing his will. So if you want to live the best life with God, that is, to give him your everything, then do it and don't be afraid of the consequences. Jesus said, 'I came to give you *life*, and life in all its fullness.' If you haven't got abundant life, then check out your faith in God and where it has taken you these past few years. And if you can't really recall much, then it's time you started to prove to your friends and to yourself that you live by faith and not by works.

...Nobody else knows it

I think a lot of the problems dealt with in this book are the problems of new Christians. Because if you still have this problem of not witnessing after a few years of being a Christian, then the problem is indeed a serious one.

Anyway, whichever you are, let's talk about witnessing.

First of all, the reasons you don't witness. Basically there are two reasons. (1) you don't know people *well* enough to feel comfortable talking about Jesus, and (2) you know people *too well* to feel comfortable talking to them about Jesus. It's not that you don't want to, and you're certainly not ashamed of being a Christian, it's just that, well, people might not understand. . . .

It's a good thing to recognize a problem in your life before it goes too far. (They say that if you think you're insane then you're *not*, because when you are, you don't know about it!) And I remember very well recognizing this particular problem of 'not witnessing' myself. The time I realized I was coming unstuck was when I first joined BBC Radio One as Assistant Publicity Officer. My job often included popping down to the studios while the DJs were on the air, and I found that when my boss Rodney said, 'Take this down to DLT,' I would find myself inadvertently taking off my 'Jesus' sticker as I wandered down the corridor. Now my Jesus stickers were my constant companions, and I loved to wear them, but I knew that they drew attention. But I also found the fact that I took them off in dodgy circumstances very annoying indeed. So in the end I had a quiet word with myself and decided that all this pulling wool over people's eyes was pathetic and that I would either carry on marching forward with banner waving in front—or I would forget the whole thing.

I don't know if you ever talk to yourself like that—but I was more than disappointed in the way my witnessing life was going. So I agreed to go the whole hog and become a banner-waving Christian, and by that I don't mean a 'weirdo', or an embarrassing fanatic, but just a person who thinks enough of her faith to want to share it with other people.

The next part of my plan then was to get rid of the stickers in favour of patches that had to be sewn on and were quite unremovable! And they did just what I said—they attracted the attention of just about everybody I met. I was amazed how interested people were in what little ol' me had to say about my faith in Jesus Christ. If you've ever been thrown on stage or classroom floor and found yourself faced with an audience, then you'll know that you have to do one of two things—do or die! And personally I've found it better to do! People think a lot more of you for standing up for your faith.

I heard very recently of a college in Wales where the Christians were treated as a big joke, and the main reason behind the joke was their fish badges. Apparently all the Christians wore these badges on the *reverse* side of their lapels, and every time a Christian passed a fellow Christian they would turn their lapels up and flash these badges at each other. Very reminiscent of 'The Famous Five' and other secret societies that were very much part of my childhood—but not really college material, eh? Anyone would think that we had all gone underground and were being tortured à la Iron Curtain. But happily for us there is no persecution and anyone can proclaim Jesus Christ as Lord! Even you!

Of course all arguments stop at this next paragraph:

'Be wise in the way you act towards those who are not believers, making good use of every opportunity you have. Your speech should always be pleasant and interesting, and you should know how to give the right answer to everyone' (Colossians 4:5-6).

I love this particular passage of Scripture because it is so straightforward. No hidden meanings, just down-the-line teaching. The more you read it, the more you realize what a tall order it is. 'Making good use of every opportunity.'

Now, you can't make an opportunity happen, you can't really plan opportunities. They usually happen to you. A chance meeting is an opportunity; so is someone asking you why you're wearing a 'God loves you' badge.

And if you think that you haven't got a good enough vocabulary and you can't phrase things very well, I'm afraid you are just made for the job as far as Paul is concerned. All it needs from you is a friendly straightforward chat. And if you can only speak in words of one syllable, then the chances are that people will understand you better anyway.

Okay, so let's look at ways in which you can help to tell other people about Jesus.

Open Airs I wonder if you shudder at the thought of this. An open air can be the biggest disaster or the greatest success, depending on how you go about it. I think that to put on an effective open air meeting, it must *not* be spontaneous! An open air needs a great deal of planning. I wonder how many times you've been to an open air where half the people who said that they would turn up and help . . . just never appeared? A lot of the time they are too ashamed to admit that they belong to this motley crew of people who don't really know what they are doing.

Now, what I want *you* to do is to organize a really good open air, and you can do it! Get the young people of your church together for a special meeting (use your youth meeting night if you can, because then you're not dragging them out on an extra night). Together you plan a format, making full use of music. Something like this: Group—two songs/everybody—one song/intro by Pete/repetitive chorus by all/group—two songs/5-minute testimony by Sally/solo singer—one song/5-minute sketch by Dave and Ron/group—one song/5-minute testimony by Debbie/one last song by everyone/home.

Now, that will take about an hour, which is plenty long enough. We're not in a competition to see who can hold the longest meetings. It doesn't prove that you're more spiritual than anyone else—or more dedicated come to that!

So, you've got your programme. But that's not it, that's just the start. Now you start the rehearsal! Rehearsal? Yes! If you want to show people that you have something to offer them, then it must be put in an attractive and professional wrapper. That's what people are used to! Rehearsing can be great fun; we did it at our church and really had a good time. The idea is that everything in your programme follows on smoothly, and once you've been through it a couple of times you will feel so much more confident about facing people in the street. The other beauty of having a programme is that it can be duplicated and given out in the street. The duplicated leaflet should contain the programme, plus words of any songs that are worth joining in, plus an invitation to your church or churches and, of course, a very simple gospel message. By giving people this leaflet, they will be able to see for themselves what is going on, and if they don't like the preaching they may still wait around to hear the group sing again! That way, you keep them for the whole open air! We tried this, and it really worked well—in fact, we blocked the street and the police tried to move us on, until they found out we had permission to be there! So you can be a very effective witness for Jesus, if you take time to work it out properly!

Street Witnessing Door to Door Talking to people you don't know is hard. In fact, if you *can* just walk up to someone in the street and start up a full-scale conversation with them, then you are gifted in a very special way. For most of us, it's hard work! I mean, what do you say to someone who you've not only never met, but haven't even been introduced to? Your first answer is in the question. Introduce yourself! Tell them your first name and the church you belong to; that's enough for them to sum up that you are going to try and draw them into a 'religious' conversation. If your person isn't interested, then he will withdraw there and then, but if he hangs around for the next sentence, you can take it that he is at least mildly interested.

The best way to chat is to ask questions. That way you get a two-way conversation going! That's why a survey is always a good idea. Again, this helps you all to get together and decide on a subject for the survey, such as: 'Why do people go to church?' or, 'How many people in the town believe there is a life after death?' This of course would just be your theme, so then you need a list of questions, preferably the sort that *can't* be answered by 'Yes' or 'No'. Surveys are fun, and give a great change for people who may never have witnessed in this way before.

Press and Radio Everyone wishes that there was more on the radio about Christianity, but the only reason there isn't is that nobody does anything about it! When was the last time you told your local radio station about some event at your local church? It has to be newsworthy, of course, but the next time you have a well-known speaker or artiste appearing at your church, notify your radio station. I mean, have you heard some of the rubbish they churn out on the local stations? Stories of how Mr Jones down the street has grown the biggest marrow in the whole of the village! Or how the police have been called in on two more outbreaks of petty theft at the local grocer's. It's not exactly dynamic news, is it? So when you've been out on your survey . . . why not send them the results? Tell them of the general reaction. And then if they ask for someone to interview, make sure it's someone in authority, who can use the opportunity to the best advantage. And do the same thing with the press. When you have a rally of a sizable degree, don't just send in the usual advertisement for them to print. Write them a press release, giving all the details and making it as interesting as you can. You'll be surprised how many times the press and radio will use your stories!

Coffee Bars In some towns they are considered old-hat, but the majority of times they go down extremely well—though again, they need a great deal of organization. We used to hold one called 'The Spontaneous Christian Coffee Bar'. Now, the title of that gives you the idea that nothing was organized, whereas in reality nothing could be further from the truth! The basic idea was to have a place where Christians could meet for nothing more than a social evening. We just put on a few coloured lights, laid on coffee and refreshments, spread a few tables around and had records playing quietly in the background. People came just to sit and chat with each other, because there was nowhere else to go, so we were supplying a need in the Christian community. Eventually, as the evening wore on, someone would pick up a guitar and start strumming a few choruses, and maybe people would join in. By the end of the evening it wouldn't be unusual to find ourselves in the middle of a time of praise and worship.

The organization behind the evening wasn't the usual type. We had to create an informal atmosphere, and that wasn't easy! So we had a few people to play these guitars now and again, just in the background so that they weren't interfering with anything—although if it happened to take off, so much the better. We asked people to come along with something prepared, like a sketch or a song, but they also had to be prepared *not* to use it! So although it was organized—it wasn't, if you see what I mean!

Ah! But the moral behind the story was this: we had more Christians bringing their unsaved friends to that than to most things, because they realized that their friends were not going to get preached at. The atmosphere, however, spoke for itself, and through it people came to the church, while some even gave their lives to Christ in the coffee bar itself.

There are umpteen ways of witnessing, and if you feel too shy to take it all on yourself, then try a few of the ways I've mentioned. Because the more you witness, the easier it will become for you, and you'll soon find yourself doing it even when you've not got it organized!

..I can't stand Jenny!

'Every test that you have experienced is the kind that normally comes to people. But God keeps his promise, and he will not allow you to be tempted beyond your power to remain firm; at the time you are put to the test, he will give you the strength to endure it, and so provide you with a way out.' (1 Corinthians 10:13).

That text is a tremendous one to learn parrot fashion and a great one to mumble under your breath when people really get up your nose! But seriously, keeping your temper under control in excruciating circumstances can be the hardest thing in the world. Before I was a Christian I had a pretty bad temper (just ask my Mum), but unfortunately I used to hit out rather than attack with words. I can always vividly remember warning someone not to touch a very valuable 78 rpm record I was carrying in a hold-all. The schoolboy in question did not heed my remarks and made straight for my bag. There followed an ear-tingling *crack!* as I walloped this poor fella round the face. The whole classroom went silent and I realized how out-of-line my temper had been. Had the boy smashed the record, maybe I might have been right to be annoyed, but as it was, the boy was just tempting me or testing me, by touching my bag.

A lot of the time our tempers are unjustified to say the least. Our feelings can be affected by the weather, by what we've eaten and hundreds of other minor circumstances. We all have days when for no apparent reason we feel grumpy or depressed and somehow we seem to disagree with everyone and everything. That's the reason why we should let God guide our lives and not rely on our feelings.

So what happens when you can't stand someone? (Apologies to anyone called Jenny, it was a name I picked out of the air!) A lot of our not liking someone is not knowing them, and in our minds we conjure up all these mental notes of what that person is like, which is totally unfair.

In June of '78 the group had the chance to go to some TV studios and watch the Holland v Scotland match being televised. It was a unique experience watching the director yelling at the commentator in Argentina down one mike, and telling Brian Moore he only had 30 seconds before the adverts came on in another mike, and other people shouting out count-downs. The whole studio was highly organized chaos! On this particular day, the studio panel included Brian Clough, and somehow I have always expected him to be a very sharp, impatient person. Yet he turned out to be an extremely nice guy, with plenty of time to chat and sign autographs. Poor Brian Clough had virtually been condemned without a trial!

Love is a *fruit* of the Spirit. It is not a gift, so don't try to argue that you just haven't got it in you to love certain people. There are people in your life that you must find almost impossible to like, let alone love, and yet the Bible tells us it is possible to love everyone!

Let's talk about love being a fruit of the Spirit. First and foremost, if you are a born-again Christian then God's Spirit is alive in you, and that means that you are able to bear fruit. But fruit doesn't just appear. An apple tree can take years before it starts bearing fruit, and even when it does, it doesn't all of a sudden one morning have huge rosy apples on it! No, it starts with apple blossom and then gradually a very small sour green apple appears. As the fruit grows it becomes bigger and sweeter.

I'm sure by now you can see what I'm getting at. Love is a fruit that needs to grow, and as you grow in your knowledge and love of the Lord so your love for others will grow too.

I'd like to tell you of someone in whom the fruit of love is growing very nicely.

When I married John, he was a minister in a church in the East End of London, and I was a member of a church in Barking, Essex. Bringing, or rather introducing a wife into a church when the congregation was used to having a single minister is a bit traumatic, and there was an atmosphere of resentment for quite a while. Then one day we were just about to begin a meeting when one of our ladies stood up and walked to the front. We wondered what was going on, when she said, 'Before this meeting goes any further, I feel there is something I should say.' What followed was a statement I'll never forget. She confessed that since I had been in the church she had resented my presence and found it hard to accept me, a stranger, as the wife of their minister. But the Lord had been dealing with her, and she said she realized that it was totally the wrong attitude and that through the Lord breaking her down she was now able to say that she loved me. She asked that others come forward to say the same. Nobody did, and I can't say I blame them, for what that lady did was so unusual and so highly commendable that I don't think I could have done it myself. But what fruit!! To be able to stand up before a congregation and right a wrong like that! From that moment on the atmosphere relaxed and I enjoyed the remainder of my time there with everybody, because her statement caused us all to sit up and think.

A lot of the time the Lord himself deals with this problem of hate or intense dislike. I can remember being in a Bible study when the minister said how wrong it was to say, 'I'll never speak to that person again!' He was talking from the verse, 'Repay no man evil for evil'. There was a lady in the meeting who had just come in, and as she had been walking down the street she had been complaining to her friend about a relation. Her very words had been 'I'll never speak to her again!' So once more I was a witness to someone stopping a meeting to confess a weakness: this time the lady involved had seen the folly of what she had said. When she went home she did something about it! That's very important. When God teaches us a lesson, it's just as well to obey it and follow it through! It's easy, of course, to 'love' everyone when things are going well, such as when you first become a Christian: everything is *so* beautiful, every*one* is *so* beautiful, rain is beautiful, thunder is beautiful, everything that was ever horrible is beautiful! You forgive people with overwhelming grace, you throw yourself into everything without sparing a thought for yourself, and the Lord gets a decent percentage of your time because you are so grateful that he died for you.

And talking of Jesus dying for you. . . . If you ever forget what it is to love—just look at what Jesus did. We get very, very familiar with the story of salvation, of the wonderful story of the sacrifice of one pure life in exchange for ours, but salvation is what love is all about. Never get tired of that. When you pray, it's good to start by going over God's plan in Jesus, how he lived for you, died for you and rose again so that you would also rise and live with him for ever. Once you've started to go over the ultimate Love Story, you begin to see again what love is all about, and there's nothing quite like love to make you stop hating!

Sometimes it's good to laugh at yourself, when you get into a circumstance where you are raving mad at someone or something. When Dunamis first started touring, we found there were certain things that annoyed us. Perhaps one week we would have trouble starting our van and we'd all start screaming at it: 'C'mon Aggie! You can make it! Oh for goodness' sake Aggie *start*! Oh good grief how did we get lumbered with this lump of scrap metal. . . .' And then gradually the silly comments would start. 'Why didn't we pray for a Rolls Royce? We might not have been able to get the equipment in it, but at least it would start! I've seen Hillman Imps start better than this! Well, if the van's not going to start, we'll have to have an open air right here—someone phone the head-master and tell him to bring the fourth formers out to the High Road. . . .'

I don't know if you've ever watched *Fawlty Towers* on TV, but there was one sketch where John Cleese couldn't get a car to start. He got so mad, he started hitting the bonnet with a twig. It was so pathetic, but very very funny. And that's how we must look at times, when we get annoyed and frustrated.

As a group, we realized how futile it was to shout at the van, but it never stopped us doing it. And then once, when we were in Wales, we came across a certain gate outside a church car park. This particular gate would not keep open by itself, and needed two people to manoeuvre it. One to hold the gate back, and the other to stop the loose bits of rusty wire from scratching the van. We were there for a week, and every time we went to the church we had to drive up to this silly gate, get out and go through the rigmarole of fighting with the wire. And then on the way out, we would all get in the van and forget that the gate had to be opened once more. By the end of the week, all our wrath had descended on that gate! All the wrath that usually went on the van was transferred to the gate.

Then a few weeks later a vital part of our P.A. equipment decided to play up while we were performing, and so the wrath from the van and the gate was poured out into our monitor speaker. Although all of this was done in fun and our so-called 'wrath' was wreathed in cheeky grins, it does give you a good idea of how a little dislike can mount up into something too big to handle. It's a good thing to give your arguments and frustrations to the Lord before you get to a stage where you're messing up your spiritual life. It says in the Bible that 'if we confess our sins to God, he will keep his promise and do what is right: he will forgive us our sins and purify us from all our wrongdoing' (1 John 1:9). It does you good to acknowledge the fact that you've sinned, and as you confess a dislike to the Lord, he often shows you just how silly you are being. Even as you give him your list of excuses for not liking someone, he will show you how petty those things are. You may be able to tell anyone in the world that you don't like so and so because . . . and the reasons will sound feasible. But when you come up against a just God, you come up against a mirror, and you see yourself as you really are; all reasoning fades away as you converse with the pure and holy Son of God.

Having a minister for a husband, I hear a lot of hair-raising stories of the good old Bible College days. Sorry, I don't intend to give away too many secrets, but there are rumours of cold baths, pillow fights, the shaving off of moustaches while students were asleep, not to mention missing mattresses and unrelenting mimicry of lecturers! But above all, there was a kind of bond between students living so closely together. When you are thrust into a bedroom along with half a dozen other students (probably all of them totally unknown to you) you will soon find that they have irritating habits and funny ways. Having to share a room with the world's most untidy person when you are ultra-neat must have its problems. Yet it's at such times that you find out a lot about yourself as well. Have you any idea how annoying you are to other people!? You think it's only them that have annoying ways. They are the only ones who snore, or use a hairdryer every morning while you're trying to sleep. . . . Well, maybe they can't stand the way you keep reading bits of your book aloud to them, or the way you must try and explain the dream you had the night before! Petty? No, not to the person you're annoying. That's why there has to be a lot of give and take . . . and it's no good 'putting up with it'; you have to love that person *with* their faults, and the sooner you do it the better. There's a common expression (I'm not sure if it's biblical, but it's good!) that says,

'Every time you point a finger at someone, there are three fingers pointing back at you!' In other words—you're not so great yourself!

Any kind of hate is bad. You know that, because it leaves a nasty taste in your mouth. You can't hate someone without it having an effect on your life. It's bound to make you disagreeable and hard to cope with and therefore it's bad for you . . . and that's a good enough reason for staying away from it!

...I'm not baptized in the Spirit

So you haven't achieved all your badges, huh? Oh, didn't you know? There's a badge for getting saved, a badge for being baptized in water, a badge for Sunday-school teacher and lots, lots more. But the Super-badge is for being baptized in the Spirit!

Sorry, yes, I am being silly, but sometimes people talk about Christian things as if you *win* then in a competition. For example: 'I play the piano every other Sunday now!' What an achievement! And people often look down on the floor and twist their fingers and finally blurt out, 'I'm not baptized in the Spirit'—as if they are admitting some great social failing and therefore will remain an embarrassment to their friends for ever.

Well, it's not like that! Not at all! There is no way you win, earn or even deserve *anything* that

God's got for you. Did you win salvation? No, of course you didn't, so why try to win the baptism in the Spirit? The Lord gave you your salvation: 'God's free gift is eternal life' (Romans 6:23). There was a time, however, when you even tried to win *that*, wasn't there? Do you remember, perhaps, trying to find God by pleading with him, by trying to be good, and then when you finally found him he had his arms open ready to welcome you. It was all so much more simple than you'd expected. You just admitted your need for him to save you from your sins and asked him to come into your life. And he did. No problem.

So how come when you want to be baptized in the Spirit you start pleading and trying to be nice again? It's a gift, like salvation. Listen to this: 'On the last and most important day of the festival Jesus stood up and said in a loud voice, "Whoever is thirsty should come to me and drink. As the scripture says, 'Whoever believes in me, streams of life-giving water will pour out from his heart.'" Jesus said this about the Spirit, which those who believed in him were going to receive. At that time the Spirit had not yet been given, because Jesus had not been raised to glory.' (John 7:37-39).

And this: 'And so I say to you: Ask, and you will receive; seek, and you will find; knock, and the door will be opened to you. For everyone who asks will receive, and he who seeks will find, and the door will be opened to anyone who knocks. Would any of you who are fathers give your son a snake when he asks for fish? Or would you give him a scorpion when he asks for an egg? Bad as you are, you know how to give good things to your children. How much more, then, will the Father in heaven give the Holy Spirit to those who ask him!' (Luke 11:9-13).

So it is a gift, and yet we still get hung up about it. We still feel we need some qualifications before it will happen to us. Here's a list of excuses we commonly chant out.

'I'm not good enough' And you never will be! We won't be like Jesus until we see him face to face, and here again we are back to the problem of trying to earn God's favour. When Peter went to see Cornelius (Acts 10), it says that the people of his household were saved and received the Spirit the same day—the same moment in fact! Now, they could never become 'good enough' in that short space of time, and yet the Bible clearly states that the Spirit was poured out on all of them. We can take it, then, that you don't need to be 'good enough' either.

'I'm scared of making a fool of myself' Yes, I know you've heard about all these people who were baptized while going down the road on a bike, or who danced down the church and climbed up the walls!! Maybe you've even *seen* someone frantically waving their arms and yelling at the top of their voice, and at the time you thought, 'Never! I'll never let that happen to me!' Listen, God gave you a personality, a character of your own. He knows what you are like, and if you are not the sort to be expressive, then you won't be. On the other hand, if you are easily excitable then maybe you *will* jump up and down. The thing is, it

is all entirely up to you! God doesn't hypnotize you so that you don't know what you are doing; you are always in full control. That means you can speak in tongues at will. It also means that there is never any need for you to think that you must leap up in the middle of a meeting and scream out a message in tongues because you just can't control yourself. Those folk that you've seen 'making fools of themselves' have done so purely because they wanted to! Most of the time they are abusing the gift rather than adding anything to it. Remember, *you* are in control!

'How can I speak a language I don't know?' You can't! That's why it's a miracle! Nobody can speak in a tongue that is foreign to them. If you could, there would be no faith in being baptized in the Spirit. What you are actually going to do in being baptized is to take a step of faith and bypass your mind!

1 Corinthians 14:14 says: 'For if I pray in this way, my spirit prays indeed, but my mind has no part in it.' Talking in tongues involves the depths of your being speaking to the depths of God, and your mind is left out of it. You will *not* understand what you are saying, and because of this you will seem to be talking gibberish. But there again, what foreign language doesn't sound gibberish if you can't understand it? Your faith has to say, 'This is it! I am speaking in tongues!'

'Why should it happen to me?' To be baptized in the Spirit, the only thing you need is to be thirsty! If you are longing for the Lord to bless you in this way then you are half-way there! In the

verses we were looking at earlier in John 7, Jesus said, 'Whoever is thirsty should come to me and drink' (verse 37). So there's one reason why it should happen to you. The same chapter goes on: 'At that time the Spirit had not yet been given, because Jesus had not been raised to glory.' Jesus *has* been raised to glory now, so that's another reason why it should happen to you!

Going on to the other set of verses in Luke 11: 'everyone who asks will receive, and he who seeks will find, and the door will be opened to anyone who knocks.' These are tremendously encouraging verses to read when praying for the baptism. God's word inspires faith and so it's a good thing to read up some of these scriptures before you actually pray.

'*What is going to happen?*' Ah! The fear of the unknown! When you ask the Lord to baptize you in the Spirit, he isn't going to take hold of your tongue and start waggling it! *You* are going to speak. When the believers were baptized, in Acts 2, it says that *they* spoke as the Spirit gave them utterance.

So it's your voice, your tongue. *But* remember you are going to speak a foreign language, so once you've asked the Lord for his gift, you have to stop speaking English! It's all very pretty and everything to sit there saying 'Hallelujah! Thank you Jesus' but while you are speaking English, you can't speak another language at the same time! You can't speak English and Spanish at the same time—unless you have two voice boxes! So you have to stop speaking your own language and believe God for a new one!

It's nice if you have someone to pray for you to receive the baptism, although obviously it's not necessary—many people receive their baptism in the quietness of their own room. However, it's helpful if people pray with you, simply because they make a noise! When you pray aloud on your own, you become much more conscious of your own voice and will therefore shy away from trying out your new language, but if there are people praying in tongues around you then you aren't a spectacle when all of a sudden you join in.

Without sounding too much like a doctor or Marjorie Proops, perhaps I could advise you *not* to be so tense! A lot of people get themselves tied up in knots, terrified that nothing's going to happen (or maybe terrified that *something's* going to happen!).

You've heard that the Holy Spirit is often likened to a beautiful dove. You probably don't own a dove, but may have tried at one time or another to coax Joey or Bluey on to your finger. No doubt you found that if you flinched when he tried to land, he just flew away again. But when you calmly stood there patiently waiting for him to come, he wasn't frightened, and finally settled. Of course, if you're one of these people who can't bear birds flapping round the room, then the chances are that you will cause chaos, waving your arms about and alarming the poor budgie.

The same goes for the Holy Spirit, who is gentle and needs to be received in much the same way.

Sometimes at church, 'seeking' meetings (silly

name really—'receiving' would be better) go on for hours and hours; but I think if you haven't received anything after fifteen minutes, then you would be wise to stop. Otherwise you are just going to sit there thinking, 'There's something wrong with me—perhaps I'm not good enough.' Then all the things we've discussed earlier will come seeping back into your mind, and the knots in your stomach will begin to tie again! Keep in your mind that the baptism is a *gift*, for you to receive. You are not in a competition, you don't earn a badge and you don't have to have any qualifications. Just relax and let rivers of water flow from deep within you. Have a wonderful time, use your gift. It's not to be put on a shelf and admired, it's for your personal use, and using it every day will strengthen your Christian life to an extent where even you will notice it!

I was going to finish the chapter here, but on thinking about it, it might be as well to take a quick look at some of the other gifts of the Spirit, so that we cut out confusion about using tongues at home, tongues at church, prophecy and interpretation.

Tongues at home 'The one who speaks in strange tongues helps only himself, but the one who proclaims God's message helps the whole church' (1 Corinthians 14:4).

There is a difference between using tongues at home and using tongues in the church. As it says in this verse, speaking in tongues is of great use to you personally. Use it every day in your own quiet times, along with praying with your mind. It adds a new dimension to your prayer life, especially at times when words seem hard to find. A lot of people seem to think you only use tongues in praise, but it can be of great value when you are feeling upset and just can't express yourself any other way.

Witnessing becomes easier: there's more authority in what you say; and as I said before, even *you* will notice the difference in the strength of your Christian life!

Tongues at church '. . . but the one who proclaims God's message helps the whole church.'

To use tongues in church, you need to feel for your fellow Christians. You need to go to church thinking, 'This morning I want to be of assistance, I want to be used by God to serve my friends.' And so when you get to your church you pray, 'Lord, use me with a gift of tongues this morning, so that the church will be inspired by a message from you.' And then God will use *you* to edify the church. God uses you to bring a message of encouragement in tongues that needs to be interpreted—but we will talk about interpretation in a minute.

A message in tongues is entirely different from praising the Lord in tongues. If you jump up in the middle of a meeting and start praising God in tongues, just because you feel like it, then the only one that enters into a glory-time is you! Nobody else can understand what's going on. That's why Paul says (1 Corinthians 14:19), 'But in church worship I would rather speak five words that can be understood, in order to teach others, than speak thousands of words in strange tongues.'

At home, then, pray in tongues as much as you like, the more the merrier! In church, ask the Lord's advice first, and make sure whose glory you are doing it for!

Interpretation Again, this is something to ask the Lord for. It may be that you were praying before the service and the Lord impressed something on your mind, so that once you hear the message in tongues you just know that you have the interpretation. On the other hand you may have nothing at all, and then you will need to step out completely in faith, believing that if you ask the Lord for a *good thing*, he won't give you a stone or a serpent.

Beware of getting carried away by emotion here. It has been known for folk to use interpretation to air their own views, and obviously this is wrong! But Paul says that although maybe two or three will deliver messages in tongues, only one should interpret . . . so if you are trying to be clever and stand up to interpret a message, beware! There may be one or two more on the way, and the interpretations will probably conflict with your own 'interpretation'.

Again, make sure that you are desiring to see your church built up and that God is the centre of your reason for using this gift.

Prophecy Just a word about prophecy. This is not a gift of fortune-telling or looking to the future. Prophecy is usually encouragement or confirmation. The Lord often uses prophecy to put our minds at ease over a matter that's been worrying us. Or maybe we have needed a bit of a kick, and the Lord has told us to pull our socks up. Prophecy comes the same way as interpretation, that is by asking and receiving, but this time you have no one to 'start you off'. Now and again people see visions and explain these visions to the church. Other times God may just give someone a word, and then it is up to that person to stand up and step out in faith on that word, relying on the Lord for the rest of the prophecy.

One last word: don't expect to give a word-perfect message when you first use a gift. If the Lord impresses on you the words 'I love you', then you stand up and say, 'The Lord says he loves you.' That might not seem much to you, but someone in your church may really need to hear those few words. So don't shy away—nobody expects you to be anything other than a beginner.

The gifts are for you. Use them!

...There are lots of little problems that trouble me

It would be impossible to go through every common problem in just one book, so here's a quickie on those other things that have probably driven you mad at one time or another. . . .

Psychological problems and their healing I find this a very dodgy subject. I'm always extremely wary of anyone who tries to find super-psychological answers to everyday problems. Let's take an example. You don't like talking to people. Now, there are folk who would delve into your past and drag out every horrible situation you've ever been in, and stamp on the nearest one that seems to fit your problem. Example: when you were young, you were hit for being shy of talking to your aunty. Your aunty had brown wavy hair and so therefore ever since then you've never been able to have a conversation with anyone sporting brown wavy hair! The strange thing is that you can make yourself believe that yarn, and all of a sudden you feel 'released' because you've remembered your aunty! On very rare occasions, this kind of psychological counselling does work, if there really is a root to pull out. But most times if people aren't very good at talking to other people, it's just because they're shy! That's all! And a lot of people would read a whole world of murky pasts into it, telling you that you are basically insecure, not shy.

Mind you, it's a good game and it can be played two ways. The first way is: 'Guess the reason behind the so-called problem'; the second, probably even more annoying, is: 'Let's all revel in my problems.' Are *you* like this? I hope you're not, because one of the biggest Christian pains-in-the-neck is the person who just adores being counselled and therefore spends entire nights dreaming up new problems for other people to sweat out with them. If you are one of these unfortunates, then it might be worth reminding you that there are *real* people with extremely *real* desperate problems, who don't want to revel in them and really want them sorted out, and *you* are in the way and taking up valuable time with nothing more than self-pity and drivel.

Ouch! Did that hurt? Well, it was meant to! It's a very dangerous game, playing with other people's problems and telling them they're oppressed (when you don't really know). You could start off the kind of problem that really *does* need some sorting out. And playing with other people's emotions when there's nothing really wrong is nothing short of callous.

When you have a problem, please make sure you take it to someone in authority, preferably a minister and *not* someone 'who's ever so good at problems'. If you just need a helpful chat, then probably a happily married couple in your church would be just right. Next time you're just plain bored and feel like being counselled, spare a thought for the unmarried mum who's found Jesus as her Saviour and needs a great deal of help in her totally new life and surroundings.

Evil and Satanic things I don't want to go too deep into this subject because I don't want you getting involved. It's good to be aware that there *is* a devil, and once you've realized that, then it's good to stay out of his way. When you walk into a Christian bookshop, you may see several shelves full of books marked 'Occult'. Now you would be much better off avoiding that section and buying yourself a good spiritual book that will help you to know Jesus better. The occult is a specialized subject and not one to study unless you have very good reason to do so. It may sound very exciting, but I can promise you that any kind of involvement with the devil is terrifying and not the least bit glamorous.

'So how do I recognize anything satanic if I have no involvement with it?' A lot of people raised this same question when *The Exorcist* film came out. What they really meant was 'I want to go and see it'. Listen, if you belong to Jesus, and you are getting closer to him, then you'll know if you come across anything satanic. Your spirit will clash with the opposing spirit and you will realize that something isn't quite right, and that's enough of a signal for you to leave. The best advice I can give you about Satan is to steer clear.

My family aren't Christians . . . and they are going to be the hardest people to get across to as well! Time and time again, when it boils down to personal things (and Christianity is a very personal thing) it's much easier to talk to strangers than to close friends or family. For this reason, you want to make sure that the life of Jesus is shining through everything you do! Mum isn't going to be impressed by how many Bible verses you know, but she will be impressed when you start becoming a nicer person to live with. When you start being thoughtful and helping out now and again, and your temper dies down, *then* your family will start raising their eyebrows and asking what's wrong!

Something that may give the wrong impression of what Jesus is all about is going to church too much! Yes, too much. Your parents like to see you now and again, and they will thoroughly appreciate you staying in a few nights. Otherwise it'll be the 'Oh you're not off down that church *again*' routine, which I'm sure you will be familiar with if your parents aren't Christians. That can make them hate the church just as much as the local disco, or pub, or wherever you used to hang out before. Walking round with a Bible in your hand all the time will only give you the affectionate name of 'religious maniac'. So really the best thing to do is to let them see that Jesus has changed you and that you're a better person, and then when they ask questions you'll be ready to tell them how Jesus has changed your life and how much happier you are. Don't give up on your parents—they love you very much.

It's not as good as it used to be This is what's generally known as 'backsliding'. An awful word I find, or maybe it's just badly used. People tend to say 'Oh, she's backslidden' in the same voice most people use for 'Oh, she's fatally wounded'—when, at a push, all you've done is missed the prayer meeting for a couple of weeks! There's always a certain amount of panic attached to the thought of anyone backsliding. I suppose everyone feels partly responsible.

Why do people backslide? I think a lot of people aren't sure of their salvation (see chapter 9) and were probably never saved in the beginning. I've come across quite a few people who have come out for counselling, and then, during the course of the conversation, I've realized that they have never asked Jesus into their hearts, even though they may have been professing to be Christians for years! So a lot of backsliders really had nothing to slide back from.

Other than that, you've probably just got your ticket to heaven . . . and stopped. The Christian life is very much a life of going forward. We are running forward, we are running a race (1 Corinthians 9:24-27)! In a race, you can be doing fine for three quarters of it, but if you stop before the finishing line it won't matter how well you ran earlier, you come nowhere at the end. So when you obtain salvation, you don't just sit back and enjoy the security of being saved—you get up and start growing!

The book of Revelation also puts forward another very good argument for 'why it's not as good as it used to be'. It says, 'But this is what I have against you: you do not love me now as you did at first. Think how far you have fallen! Turn from your sins and do what you did at first.' (Revelation 2:4-5). Perhaps this is what has happened to you. You've gone back on yourself and indulged in some sin, and in doing so you've taken two steps back. The first step back was to sin, but the second and more nagging step was when you realized in your heart that what you were doing was wrong! That niggling feeling has probably caused more trouble than the actual sin itself. Let's say, for instance, that you have started to swear like you used to, and every time you do it you feel *so* bad! You can't pray any more, you feel unable to witness and so your Christian life gradually slides backwards down the hill. It's not so much the swearing, but the terrible feeling of guilt! What you now have to realize is that you are forgiven! When you gave your life to Jesus he dealt with your sins, present, past and future! You have to realize that, and once you do, sin won't be such a problem to you. Instead of getting all screwed up inside about it because you can't help yourself, why not leave it with the Lord?

Confess to him how you feel (1 John 1:9) and then stop feeling low and unholy, and get on with the race! While you are sitting around moping because you are not one hundred per cent perfect —*people are going to hell*! They need you to be telling them about Jesus and if you have Jesus in your heart then it's your duty to tell others about him! Believe me, the best way to cure your blues is to lead someone to Jesus!

What about Sundays? There are many, many traditions attached to Christianity and none of them can save you! By tradition, we are non-smokers, hat-wearers, non-drinkers and Sunday-observers. One of the advantages of Britain's becoming a pagan society is that the new generation of kids, who are starting to hear about Jesus for the first time, do not have to worry about the golden rules. *They've never heard of them!* They will come to Jesus in a natural way without thinking to themselves, 'Oh, now that I'm a Christian, I mustn't do this and I mustn't do that!' They will just live to please Jesus. Being a Christian is nothing like becoming a member of any kind of club or society. There's no uniform and no rules! Once you are saved, you let Jesus take over and *he* changes you from glory into glory. I must have said it a thousand times in this book—but here I go again—you can't earn salvation.

Okay—over to Sundays. Here's what the Bible says about the sabbath (which as we all know was a Saturday but now it's a Sunday—so much for *that* tradition!): 'One person thinks that a certain day is more important than other days, while someone else thinks that all days are the same. Each one should firmly make up his own mind.

Whoever thinks highly of a certain day does so in honour of the Lord . . .' (Romans 14:5-6). And then verse 8: "If we live, it is for the Lord that we live, and if we die, it is for the Lord that we die. So whether we live or die, we *belong to* the Lord."

Now just to confuse everything, the sabbath was generally known as a day of rest. Now, be honest —when did you last have a rest on a Sunday? Sunday is the busiest day in the week for most Christians, especially Sunday-school teachers who literally go home after the morning service, wave at their dinners and fly back to church for Sunday school, rush around taking all the kids home and then run back to church with a sandwich in their mouth so that they can make it for the evening service. Followed by the after-rally at 8.15 p.m., making it at least 10.0 before they finally get home—unless of course they're counselling: then they might get home for Monday morning.

I think we've established that Sunday isn't a day of rest—but it *is* a day 'in honour of the Lord'. Sunday is a good day to set aside for the Lord. Therefore the sabbath must really be some other day. Certainly the Lord said that we should have a day of rest; that is sensible, for everyone needs a day to recuperate. But for the Christian that day isn't Sunday! I prefer to go with the man who treats every day as the Lord's day, rather than set one aside; but as the scripture says, 'Each one should firmly make up his own mind.'

As far as not spending and things go . . . Jesus was taken aback when people accused him of breaking the sabbath by healing a man's hand

(Mark 3:1-6). Mark says that Jesus was 'angry as he looked round at them, but at the same time he felt sorry for them, because they were so stubborn and wrong'. The people that Jesus was looking at were Pharisees, a hyper-religious bunch of people. Throughout the New Testament their religious ways were always a nuisance and a stumbling block to themselves.

If everyone stopped work on a Sunday, there would be no electricity, no lighting, no gas, no transport, no doctors or nurses; and because of this, you would have chaos! I always found it sad that an old man I knew had to take his van out and collect a round of people and take them to church because they would not use a bus on a Sunday! This poor chap spent the whole of Sunday providing a taxi-service. ' . . . So stubborn and wrong.'

Really, then, the Sunday thing is up to you. The Bible says it's for you to make up your own mind—and when you have, it goes on to say, 'Why do you pass judgement on your brother?' So watch out!

Christian Unions! One of the hardest things for a Christian schoolkid to do is join the Christian Union. I would think it's much the same situation at work, but I'd like to spend a little bit of time on schools right now.

Your school Christian Union is dull and boring. Everyone makes fun of it and you wouldn't touch it with a barge pole. If your C.U. isn't like that, praise the Lord! But the vast majority are.

There's not an easy answer to the problem either, because what you need to make that C.U. tick over is a really keen, madly enthusiastic, born-again Christian, with leadership qualities, who looks presentable or even nice, and who people in your school look up to. In a sentence—you need to get the head boy saved! Why C.U.s are so often run by anaemic Christians is beyond me. It's an incredibly hard thing to get a C.U. going, and it seems to me that *you* should have a go! You've always thought you could do it better than Eric, haven't you? Well, why not give the fellow a hand? Yes, that means that *you* have to be associated with *him*! Eric is having a real bad time trying to sort things out, and you won't go to his C.U. because you're cool and smart and trendy. But don't you see? *You* are the very person he needs! If *you're* so great, then you will be an inspiration to your school C.U.

You know who 'Eric' is—so get moving!

What do you do when you get there? There are two ways of bringing the Union to the attention of your schoolfriends. The first is by personal evangelism, that is, everyone working on someone and gradually bringing them along. (That means your membership goes from six to twelve, or fifteen to thirty—either way it's a jump.) The other way is to make a big splash. Get in touch with someone like Tear Fund and start some kind of appeal. Fund-raising can be tremendous fun, especially if you use some kind of sponsorship. Sponsored hand-walking, pram-racing, peanut-pushing—the sillier the better. Stick up posters, and make sure they know that the Christian Union are organizing it. Most people respond to fund-raising (just look at the Blue Peter and Magpie appeals!). Oh, and make sure that the first person you tell is your headmaster! Always make sure that he is happy with anything you're doing, because if you get him on your side, then he can be a tremendous help to you.

And naturally, if you are thinking of starting a Christian Union, even if there are only four of you, you must always tell the Head of your intention to meet once a week or whatever. And it's worth remembering that when you *do* get the unsaved coming to your meeting, they *won't* appreciate you trying to get them to sing choruses with words they don't know, about a God in whom they don't believe (as yet). Try hard to get decent interesting speakers as often as possible, plus films and groups. British Youth for Christ are good people to get in touch with—and then of course there's us, the Dunamis Roadshow!

Worship, clapping and dancing All three of these acts are scriptural! Maybe your own church isn't quite ready for them all, but basically they're fine.

Worship means a lot of different things to a lot of different people. We went to a festival of worship a little while ago and were amazed to find it was just a service made up of masses of Sankey hymns! In a sense, they were absolutely right; all the hymns were about worshipping the Lord; but nobody seemed to be actually *doing* it. It was more like a communal sing-along time.

It could be that clapping is looked down on in your church, and if this is so, you must be patient. It's no good forcing any sort of worship—that's probably why they went off it in the first place. Worship has to be voluntary. The Lord doesn't want us to give him the glory at gunpoint; he wants it to be a natural part of our lives! You want to worship? Then wait for the right part of the service and move as the Spirit moves. Be sensitive to what God is doing and saying in your church, and be ready to be in on it! If you clap in joyful hymns and choruses, do it joyfully, not out of spite for the people who don't like it. You must encourage and do everything out of love. People *know* when you love them, just as a dog knows when you're frightened of it!

Dancing? Not quite so common; in fact nowhere near as common as people would have you believe. I believe that it is very natural to dance when you're happy. Little children are never taught to dance with joy—but you give them an Easter egg or something, and they'll give you a splendid display of skipping out to the kitchen to show mum! (Had they not been holding an Easter egg they would probably have clapped too!)

So really, worship should be a natural reaction, and therefore when it is forced it becomes unsightly and meaningless and downright frustrating to the people involved. Worship, then, should be doing what comes naturally!

One Last Word

This book has been written as one person's viewpoint on an awful lot of subjects, and of course I don't expect you to agree with them all. I do pray, though that I've tackled the problems unselfishly, and as honestly as I could. I very much want to reassure ordinary everyday Christians that there is nothing *wrong* with them, that the problems they are facing are very common and not abnormal in the least! We all tend to think that our problems are unique and that nobody understands, but after doing a spot of counselling (through being a minister's wife and *not* as a hobby!) I've found that the subjects in this book are the most common.

Everyone needs more of Jesus, and the only way to get that is to get closer to him. And as you get closer to him, so all the things that bother you . . . fade away.

I hope that's the main message of *I'm A Christian But* . . . .